بسم الله الرحمن الرحيم

Birr al-Wālidayn

BEING DUTIFUL TO PARENTS

Birr al-Wālidayn

BEING DUTIFUL TO PARENTS

IMAM MUḤAMMAD
IBN ISMĀʿĪL AL-BUKHĀRĪ
(D. 256/870)

Translated by

MOHAMMED SIDDIQ AND
MUHAMMAD AMMAR SALIM

Edited with Commentary by

SHAYKH YUSUF SHABBIR

TURATH PUBLISHING

ISBN: 978-1-906949-37-2

Published by:
Turath Publishing
79 Mitcham Road London SW17 9PD
www.turath.co.uk +44 (20) 8767 3666

Author	Imam Muḥammad ibn Ismāʿīl al-Bukhārī
Translation	Mohammed Siddiq & Muhammad Ammar Salim
Editor	Amir Isap & Shaykh Yusuf Shabbir
Final Editor	Mariam Madge Conlan
General Editor	Yahya Batha

British Library Cataloguing in Publication Data
Al-Bukhārī Imam Muḥammad ibn Ismāʿīl
Birr al-Wālidayn—Being Dutiful to Parents
I. Title

Design & typesetting	ARM (www.whitethreadpress.com)
Printed by	Mega Printers, Istanbul

Distributors for UK and Europe
Azhar Academy Ltd.
54–56 Little Ilford Lane, London E12 5QA
trade@azharacademy.com
www.azharacademy.com

Distributors for South Africa
Darul-Ihsan Research and Education Centre
www.darulihsan.com

﴿وَوَصَّيْنَا الْإِنْسَانَ بِوَالِدَيْهِ إِحْسَانًا﴾

'And We have enjoined upon man
to do good to his parents.' (46:15)

~

Shaykh as-Saʿdī ﷺ said,

'Being good to parents means treating
them kindly in all ways; in word and in deed.'
(*Taysīr*, p.57)

Contents

Publisher's Foreword

In the Name of Allah, the Most Merciful and Compassionate

I bear witness that there is no god but Allah alone, without partners, and that Muḥammad ﷺ is His servant and messenger. I invoke the blessings of Allah and peace upon His final Messenger, Muḥammad, his family, Companions and all those who follow them in goodness till the Day of Rising.

The special standing of parents and the respect and obedience due to them are enshrined in Islam as fundamental values that reflect our sincerity and gratitude towards Allah and form the foundations of a right-guided Ummah. Imam Bukhārī's treatise, *Birr al-Wālidayn*, serves as a pointed reminder of this, by presenting hadiths on the many facets of being dutiful to parents, the virtuousness of doing so, its reward and the consequences for someone who fails to do so, as well as the obligation to maintain broader family ties.

The reader will find lessons of insight and value for a changing world, such as the onus upon Muslims to be dutiful even towards non-Muslim parents, the importance of obtaining parental permission and blessing for actions we undertake for the sake of Allah and the excellence of showing kindness towards those loved by our parents. These are values that should inform all our dealings, but sincerity dictates that they apply to our parents first and foremost. Above all, we should keep in mind that caring for our parents is a blessing and an opportunity, as a number of the hadiths in *Birr al-Walidayn* inform us. We, therefore, ask Allah, as He teaches us in the Qur'an, '*My Lord, have mercy on them, as they raised me when I was small.*' Qur'an (17:24).

We should also be mindful that parents have a responsibility to raise their children correctly in order for them to be dutiful in return, and this must start from a young age. This includes monitoring how children spend their time and the company they keep, to ensure that they stay on the right path. Small things make a difference and can have a profound effect on the next generation, so a child who is accustomed to witnessing benevolence by their parents is more likely to behave in the same manner towards them. In this regard, we ask Allah, '*Our Lord, grant us spouses and progeny that are comfort to our eyes.*' Qur'an (25:74).

All praise if for Allah. Thereafter, I would like to thank both Shaykh Mohammed Siddiq and Shaykh Muhammad Ammar Salim for bringing this indispensable work to our attention and for their contributions to its translation. May Allah reward them both. In addition, Shaykh Muhammad Ammar Salim compiled the chains of transmission for each hadith, together with biographical information on the narrators, which the reader will find as an appendix to the main text. We are grateful to Mawlānā Amir Isap and all who contributed to editing the translation. Special thanks is due to Mufti Yusuf Shabbir for his expert supervision of the translation and editing and for providing insightful commentary on each chapter. Thanks also to Mariam Madge Conlan for bringing the work to its final format. I pray that Allah accepts the efforts of all involved and makes it a means for our forgiveness and an inspiration for all those who read it. May He raise us on the Day of Judgement with those whom he has forgiven totally and enter us into the Garden with our beloved Prophet ﷺ, along with our family, teachers and friends. Ameen.

YAHYA BATHA
London 2019

Introduction

In the name of Allah, the Most Merciful, the Ever Kind.

All praise belongs to Allah, Lord of the universe and Master of our fortunes, and may peace and blessings descend upon His beloved Prophet Muḥammad ﷺ, his Companions and all those who follow in their footsteps.

Imam Bukhārī (d. 256/870) is one of the most distinguished scholars of hadith in Islamic history. His *Ṣaḥīḥ* is regarded as the most authentic book after the Qur'an and has an unprecedented level of acceptance. His credentials have been attested to by his teachers, contemporaries, students and scholars of later generations. Such is his status that our teacher, Muḥaddith al-ʿAṣr (Hadith Master of the era) Shaykh Muḥammad Yūnus Jownpūrī (d. 1438/2017), suggests that Imam Bukhārī is a unique miracle of Prophet Muḥammad ﷺ that manifested two centuries after the Prophetic era. In addition to his *Ṣaḥīḥ*, Imam Bukhārī authored more than twenty books, many of which are published.

One of the books authored by Imam Bukhārī is *Birr al-Wālidayn*, a short treatise on being dutiful to parents. The treatise was published a few years ago by Dār al-Ḥādīth al-Kattāniyyah, based on a manuscript found in the personal collection of the erudite Moroccan scholar Ḥāfiẓ ʿAbd al-Ḥayy al-Kattānī (d. 1382/1962). Prior to its publication, it was assumed that the book no longer exists. When our respected teacher, Muḥaddith al-ʿAṣr Shaykh Muḥammad Yūnus Jownpūrī, received a copy of the book, he began to kiss it out of happiness and joy, reflecting his life-long attachment and devotion to Imam Bukhārī and his works. This scene was witnessed by my respected father Mufti Shabbīr Aḥmad (b. 1376/1957), who suggested to me that the treatise should be translated into English for the benefit of the wider public.

My dear and beloved student Mawlānā Moḥammed Siddīq agreed to undertake this task and the result is this publication before you.

This treatise of Imam Bukhārī is a small collection of 75 hadiths transmitted under various chapter headings. The collection focuses on two broad themes which we have categorised into two sections: firstly, the hadiths pertaining to being dutiful to parents, and secondly, the hadiths pertaining to maintaining broader family ties. The final hadith transmitted by Imam Bukhārī relates to the first theme, perhaps reminding the reader of the primary purpose of this book.

It is worth noting that Imam Bukhārī has dedicated several chapters within the Book of Manners in his *Ṣaḥīḥ* to both these themes. Likewise, he has a standalone publication, *Al-Adab al-Mufrad*, which has many more chapters and hadiths pertaining to both these themes. Thus, most of the hadiths transmitted in this short collection have also been transmitted by Imam Bukhārī in one or both of these books, as readers will gauge from the referencing (*takhrīj*) of the hadiths in the footnotes. In addition, there are several narrations on the subject matter which have been transmitted in *Ṣaḥīḥ al-Bukhārī* and/or *Al-Adab al-Mufrad* but have not been transmitted in this collection. The translations of these narrations have therefore been added as appendices to this book for the benefit of readers.

In relation to the format of this translation, readers should note the following. Firstly, the chains of transmission have been omitted, as the original Arabic publication can be referred to for this. Secondly, repeated narrations within the same chapter have been omitted. However, some repeated narrations have been retained if they appear within different chapters, particularly if Imam Bukhārī has used the narration to make a different deduction, or if the *matn* (text) of the narration is different. Thirdly, brief notes have been added to the narrations and chapter headings. Imam Bukhārī's rationale for transmitting certain narrations which do not appear to have any link with the subject matter of the book has also been addressed. Fourthly, the referencing of Dār al-Ḥadīth al-Kattāniyyah has been used, albeit with a few minor numeric tweaks.

What makes this collection unique is that Imam Bukhārī appears to be the first person to pen a discreet treatise on being dutiful to parents. Several scholars after him followed suit. They include: Imam Ibrāhīm al-Ḥarbī (d. 285/898–9), Imam Qāsim ibn al-Aṣbagh al-Qurṭubī (d. 340/951), Imam Abū ash-Shaykh al-Aṣbahānī (d. 369/979) and others.

We pray to Almighty Allah to forgive our shortcomings and make this collection a means of guidance and salvation in both worlds. May Allah bless the lives of our parents and make us and our progenies the coolness of their eyes, and unite us all in Paradise.

YUSUF SHABBIR, BLACKBURN
1 Rajab 1439/17 March 2018

SECTION 1

Being Dutiful to Parents

بَاب: قَوْلُ اللهِ تَعَالَى:
﴿وَوَصَّيْنَا الْإِنْسَانَ بِوَالِدَيْهِ حُسْنًا﴾

Chapter: The speech of Allah the Exalted: 'And We instructed Man to be good to his parents.' Qur'ān (31:14)

HADITH 1

عن أَبِيْ عَمْرٍو الشَّيْبَانِيِّ يَقُوْلُ: أَخْبَرَنَا صَاحِبُ هَذِهِ الدَّارِ، وَأَوْمَأَ بِيَدِهِ إِلَى دَارِ عَبْدِ اللهِ يَعْنِيْ ابْنَ مَسْعُوْدٍ ﵁ قَالَ: سَأَلْتُ النَّبِيَّ ﷺ أَيُّ الْعَمَلِ أَحَبُّ إِلَى اللهِ تَعَالَى؟ قَالَ: الصَّلاَةُ عَلَى وَقْتِهَا، قُلْتُ: ثُمَّ أَيٌّ؟ قَالَ: ثُمَّ بِرُّ الْوَالِدَيْنِ، قُلْتُ: ثُمَّ أَيٌّ؟ قَالَ: الْجِهَادُ فِي سَبِيلِ اللهِ، قَالَ: حَدَّثَنِيْ بِهِنَّ، فَلَوِ اسْتَزَدْتُهُ لَزَادَنِيْ.

Abū ʿAmr ash-Shaybānī said, 'The owner of this house informed us,' and he pointed with his hand to the house of ʿAbdullāh, referring to Ibn Masʿūd ﵁, "I asked the Prophet ﷺ, 'Which action is most beloved to Allah the Exalted?' He replied, 'Prayer performed on time.' I asked, 'Then what?' He said, 'Then being dutiful to parents.' I asked, 'Then what?' He said, 'Jihad in the path of Allah.'" He [Ibn Masʿūd ﵁] said, "He related these things to me, and if I had asked him further, he would have told me more."[1]

1 *Ṣaḥīḥ al-Bukhārī* (527, 2782, 5970), *Al-Adab al-Mufrad* (1), *Ṣaḥīḥ Muslim* (85).

HADITH 2

عَنِ ابْنِ مَسْعُوْدٍ ﵁ قَالَ: قَالَ رَسُوْلُ اللهِ ﷺ: أَفْضَلُ الْاَعْمَالِ أوِ الْعَمَلِ الصَّلَاةُ لِوَقْتِهَا وَبِرُّ الْوَالِدَيْنِ.

Ibn Masʿūd ﵁ narrates, 'The Messenger of Allah ﷺ said, "The most virtuous of deeds (or: the most virtuous deed) is the prayer performed on time and being dutiful to parents."'[1]

HADITH 3

عَنِ عَبْدِ اللهِ ﵁ قَالَ: قَالَ رَسُوْلُ اللهِ ﷺ: أَفْضَلُ الْعَمَلِ الصَّلَاةُ لِوَقْتِهَا وَالْجِهَادُ فِيْ سَبِيْلِ اللهِ.

ʿAbdullāh [Ibn Masʿūd] ﵁ narrates, 'The Messenger of Allah ﷺ said, "The most virtuous deed is the prayer performed on time and jihad in the path of Allah."' *Shuʿab al-Īmān* (3910).

HADITH 4

عَنِ ابْنِ مَسْعُوْدٍ ﵁ قَالَ: سَأَلْتُ النَّبِيَّ ﷺ: أَيُّ الْأَعْمَالِ أَفْضَلُ؟ قَالَ: اَلصَّلَاةُ وَبِرُّ الْوَالِدَيْنِ وَالْجِهَادُ فِيْ سَبِيْلِ اللهِ، وَلَوِ اسْتَزَدْتُهُ لَزَادَنِيْ.

Ibn Masʿūd ﵁ narrates, 'I asked the Prophet ﷺ, "Which actions are most virtuous?" He said, "The prayer [performed on time], being dutiful to parents and jihad in the path of Allah." And if I had asked further, he would have told me more.' *Musnad Aḥmad* (3973), *Al-Muʿjam al-Kabīr* (9817, 9818).

Commentary: Ḥāfiẓ Ibn Rajab (d. 795/1393) has provided an elaborate explanation of these narrations in *Fatḥ al-Bārī* (4:211), concluding that

1 Ibid.

from the rights of Allah upon His servants, prayer (*ṣalāh*) is the most virtuous; from the rights of servants to each other, being dutiful to parents is the most virtuous; and from the optional deeds, jihad is the most virtuous. The hadith, therefore, encompasses all three facets of the Faith. Indeed, ʿAllāmah Ibn Ḥazm (d. 456/1064) suggests there is scholarly consensus on the obligation of being dutiful to parents. (*Al-Ādāb ash-Sharʿiyyah*, 1:437)

ʿAllāmah Ibn Baṭṭāl (d. 449/1057) suggests in *Sharḥ Ṣaḥīḥ al-Bukhārī* (2:157) that the mention of dutifulness to parents alongside *ṣalāh* demonstrates its importance and virtue. He further draws a comparison with the verse of the Qur'an wherein Allah Almighty says:

﴿أَنِ اشْكُرْ لِي وَلِوَالِدَيْكَ﴾

Be grateful to Me and to both your parents. Qur'an (31:14).

ʿAllāmah Ibn Baṭṭāl, at another juncture, *Sharḥ Ṣaḥīḥ al-Bukhārī*, 9:188. makes reference to the verse of the Qur'an wherein Allah Almighty says:

﴿وَقَضَىٰ رَبُّكَ أَلَّا تَعْبُدُوا إِلَّا إِيَّاهُ وَبِالْوَالِدَيْنِ إِحْسَانًا﴾

And your Lord has commanded that you shall not worship anyone but Him, and show kindness to parents. Qur'an (17:23).

It is worth noting that some hadiths on the most virtuous or most beloved act to Allah appear contradictory, as some make reference to being dutiful to parents, the performance of prayer on time and jihad, whilst others suggest the remembrance of Allah and Hajj. Various explanations have been offered by hadith experts to reconcile the narrations. One explanation is that the Prophet ﷺ provided different answers to different Companions on account of their individual circumstance; for example, Ibn Masʿūd ؓ had a mother. Alternatively, the different answers were provided to address the specific need of the Muslims at the time, such as jihad; or because the time of the year, such as the Hajj season, necessitated a different answer. (*Al-Kawākib ad-Dirārī*, 4:182; *Fatḥ al-Bārī*, 2:9).

بَاب: يَبَرُّ الْوَالِدَ الْمُشْرِكَ مَا لَمْ يَأْمُرْ بِمَعْصِيَةٍ

Chapter: Being dutiful to a polytheist parent as long as they do not instruct one to sin

HADITH 5

عَنْ مُصْعَبِ بْنِ سَعْدٍ عَنْ أَبِيهِ سَعْدِ بْنِ أَبِيْ وَقَّاصٍ ﷺ قَالَ: نَزَلَتْ فِيَّ أَرْبَعُ آيَاتٍ مِنْ كِتَابِ اللهِ عَزَّ وَجَلَّ: حَلَفَتْ أُمِّيَ أَنْ لَا تَأْكُلَ وَلَا تَشْرَبَ حَتَّى تُفَارِقَ مُحَمَّدًا ﷺ، فَأَنْزَلَ اللهُ تَعَالَى: ﴿وَإِنْ جَاهَدَاكَ عَلَى أَنْ تُشْرِكَ بِيْ مَا لَيْسَ لَكَ بِهِ عِلْمٌ فَلاَ تُطِعْهُمَا وَصَاحِبْهُمَا فِي الدُّنْيَا مَعْرُوفًا﴾، وَالثَّانِيَةُ: أَنِّيْ كُنْتُ أَخَذْتُ سَيْفًا فَأَعْجَبَنِيْ، فَقُلْتُ: يَا رَسُوْلَ اللهِ، هَبْ لِيْ هَذَا، فَنَزَلَتْ: ﴿يَسْأَلُوْنَكَ عَنِ الأَنْفَالِ﴾، وَالثَّالِثَةُ أَنِّيْ كُنْتُ مَرِضْتُ فَأَتَانِيْ النَّبِيُّ ﷺ، فَقُلْتُ: يَا رَسُوْلَ اللهِ، إِنِّي أُرِيْدُ أَنْ أَقْسِمَ مَالِيْ، أَفَأُوْصِي بِالنِّصْفِ؟ فَقَالَ: لَا، فَقُلْتُ: الثُّلُثُ؟ فَسَكَتَ، فَكَانَ الثُّلُثُ بَعْد جَائِزًا، وَالرَّابِعَةُ: أَنِّيْ شَرِبْتُ الْخَمْرَ مَعَ قَوْمٍ مِنَ الأَنْصَارِ، فَضَرَبَ رَجُلٌ مِنْهُمْ أَنْفِيْ بِلَحْيِ جَمَلٍ، فَأَتَيْتُ رَسُوْلَ اللهِ ﷺ، فَأَنْزَلَ اللهُ تَعَالَى تَحْرِيْمَ الْخَمْرِ.

Saʿd ibn Abī Waqqās ﷺ said, 'Four verses from the book of Allah ﷻ were revealed regarding me: [The first was when] my mother took an oath that she would neither eat nor drink until I left Muḥammad ﷺ; so Allah the Most Exalted revealed, "*And if they try to make you associate something with Me about which you have no knowledge, then do not obey them, and keep company with them courteously in the world.*" Qur'an (31:15). The second was when I took a sword which I liked and I said, "O Messenger of Allah, gift this to me;" so [the verse] was revealed: "*They ask you about the spoils of war. . .*" Qur'an (8:1). The third was when I was ill and the Prophet ﷺ came to me and I said, "O Messenger of Allah, I want to distribute my wealth, can I bequeath half?" He said, "No," so I said, "A third?" Then he remained silent, so [a bequest of] one third was permissible thereafter. The fourth was when I had been drinking wine with a group of the Helpers (*Anṣār*) and one of them hit my nose with the jawbone of a camel. I went to the Prophet ﷺ, and then Allah the Most Exalted revealed the prohibition of wine.' *Al-Adab al-Mufrad* (24), *Muslim* (1748).

Commentary: Imam Bukhārī uses the verse of the Qur'an and the occasion of revelation to affirm that a person must be dutiful to his non-Muslim parents as long as they do not instruct one to sin. The Imam transmitted a hadith in his *Ṣaḥīḥ* (5979) under the chapter, 'A married woman maintaining ties with her mother,' which is directly relevant to this chapter. Asmā' ﷺ narrates, 'My mother who was a polytheist came with her son during the period of the peace treaty with the Quraysh and their agreement with the Prophet ﷺ. I went to ask the Prophet ﷺ, saying, "Indeed, my mother has arrived and she is hoping [for my favour]." He ﷺ said, "Yes, maintain ties with your mother." Imam Bukhārī also transmits this narration in his *Ṣaḥīḥ* (2620) under the chapter 'Gifting to polytheists.'

The Ḥanafī scholar Imam Muḥammad ibn al-Ḥasan (d. 189/805) writes in his *Muwatta'* (3:375), after transmitting the narration of ʿUmar ﷺ in which he gifted a cloak to his polytheist brother in Makkah, 'There is no harm in giving a gift to a polytheist who is residing in a place which is at war with the Muslims, so long as he does not gift him a weapon or armour.'

بَاب: الْأُمُّ ثُمَّ الْأَبُ أَحَقُّ النَّاسِ بِحُسْنِ الصُّحْبَةِ

Chapter: The mother is most deserving of best companionship, then the father

HADITH 6

عَنْ أَبِي هُرَيْرَةَ ﵁ [قَالَ:] قَالَ رَجُلٌ: يَا رَسُوْلَ اللهِ، مَنْ أَحَقُّ النَّاسِ بِالصُّحْبَةِ؟ قَالَ: أُمَّكَ، قَالَ: ثُمَّ مَنْ؟ قَالَ: ثُمَّ أُمَّكَ، قَالَ ثُمَّ مَنْ؟ قَالَ: أَبَاكَ. قَالَ: فَيَرَوْنَ أَنَّ لِأُمِّكَ الثُّلُثَيْنَ وَلِأَبِيْكَ الثُّلُثُ، قِيْلَ لِسُفْيَانَ: لِلْأُمِّ الثُّلُثَانِ فِي الْحَدِيْثِ؟ قَالَ: نَعَمْ، سَمِعْتُهُ مِنِ ابْنِ شُبْرُمَةَ يُحَدِّثُ عَنْ عُمَارَةَ، قَبْلَ أَنْ أَرَاهُ، فَسَأَلْتُ عُمَارَةَ فَجَاءَ بِهِ.

Abū Hurayrah ﷺ narrates, 'A man once asked, "O Messenger of Allah, who is most deserving of [my] companionship?" He ﷺ said, "Your mother." He said, "Then who?" He ﷺ said, "Then your mother." He said, "Then who?" He [ﷺ] said, "Your father."'[1] He [i.e. Abū Hurayrah] said: 'Therefore their view is that two thirds [of good companionship] are for your mother and one third is for your father.' Sufyān was asked, 'Are two thirds for the mother in the narration?' He replied 'Yes, I heard it from Ibn Shubrumah, who narrated it from 'Umārah before I saw him; then I asked 'Umārah and he narrated it [directly to me].'

---

1 *Ṣaḥīḥ Ibn Ḥibbān* (433), *Sunan Ibn Mājah* (3658), *Sharḥ Mushkil al-Āthār* (1671).

HADITH 7

عَنْ أَبِيْ هُرَيْرَةَ ﷺ قَالَ: جَاءَ رَجُلٌ إِلَى رَسُوْلِ اللهِ ﷺ فَقَالَ: يَا رَسُوْلَ اللهِ مَنْ أَحَقُّ بِحُسْنِ صَحَابَتِيْ؟ قَالَ: أُمُّكَ، قَالَ: ثُمَّ مَنْ؟ قَالَ: أُمُّكَ، قَالَ: ثُمَّ مَنْ؟ قَالَ: أُمُّكَ، قَالَ: ثُمَّ مَنْ؟ قَالَ: أَبُوْكَ.

Abū Hurayrah ﷺ narrates, 'A man came to Allah's Messenger ﷺ and said, "O Messenger of Allah, who is most deserving of my best companionship?" He [ﷺ] replied, "Your mother." He said, "Then who?" He [ﷺ] replied, "Your mother." He said, "Then who?" He [ﷺ] replied, "Your mother." He asked [for the fourth time] "Then who?" He [ﷺ] replied, "Your father."'[1]

HADITH 8

عَنْ أَبِيْ هُرَيْرَةَ ﷺ قَالَ: قِيْلَ: يَا رَسُوْلَ اللهِ، مَنْ أَبَرُّ؟ قَالَ: أُمَّكَ، قَالَ: ثُمَّ مَنْ؟ قَالَ: أُمَّكَ، قَالَ: ثُمَّ مَنْ؟ قَالَ: ثُمَّ أُمَّكَ، قَالَ: ثُمَّ مَنْ؟ قَالَ: ثُمَّ أَبَاكَ.

Abū Hurayrah ﷺ narrates, 'It was asked, "O Messenger of Allah, who should I be most dutiful to?" He [ﷺ] replied, "Your mother." He said, "Then who?" He [ﷺ] replied, "Your mother." He said, "Then who?" He [ﷺ] replied, "Your mother." He asked [for the fourth time] "Then who?" He [ﷺ] replied, "Then your father."'[2]

Commentary: There are several points worth noting here:

Firstly, the narration transmitted in *Al-Adab al-Mufrad* (6) and other collections has the following addition, 'Then the closest [relative] to

1 *Ṣaḥīḥ al-Bukhārī* (5971), *Al-Adab al-Mufrad* (6), *Ṣaḥīḥ Muslim* (2548).

2 *Al-Adab al-Mufrad* (5). A similar narration is transmitted via another chain from another Companion in *Musnad Aḥmad* (20028, 20048), *Sunan Abī Dāwūd* (5139), *Jāmiʿ at-Tirmidhī* (1897) and other collections.

you, then the closest to you.' There is a chapter regarding this towards the end of this collection.

Secondly, the first hadith in this chapter suggests that the mother is twice as deserving of good companionship, whereas the second and third hadiths suggest the mother is three times more deserving. Imam Ṭaḥāwī (d. 321/933) suggests in *Sharḥ Mushkil al-Āthār* (1671) that the hadiths which mention threefold kindness to the mother are more authentic.

Thirdly, 'Allāmah Ibn Baṭṭāl explains in *Sharḥ Ṣaḥīḥ al-Bukhārī* (9:189) that a person should show three times more affection, kindness and love to their mother than their father. The reason for this is that the mother has undertaken three burdensome tasks that the father has not: pregnancy, giving birth and the post-natal stages of breastfeeding and childcare. For this reason, the saint (*walī*) Imam Muḥāsibī (d. 243/857) suggests that the scholars are unanimous in the mother having a greater right to kindness and obedience from her children than the father. However, Imam Mālik (d. 179/795) suggests that both parents have an equal right and that the reason for the emphasis on the mother in the hadith is because people generally do not fulfil the rights of the mother. On the other hand, Shaykh Rashīd Aḥmad Gangohī (d. 1323/1905) suggests in *Al-Kawkab ad-Durrī* (3:44) that the mother has greater right to affection and kindness, whilst the father has greater right to respect and obedience. This is broadly in line with what has been mentioned by Ḥanafī scholars (*Al-Fatāwā al-Hindiyyah* (5:365)).

Fourthly, Ḥāfiẓ Ibn al-Qayyim (d. 751/1350) makes a pertinent point in *Zād al-Ma'ād* (5:490) that being dutiful to parents does not mean that a person only supports them financially if they are unable to work or if they are in need. He adds that if a person is wealthy, yet allows his parents to undertake manual labour, such as cleaning toilets or washing people's clothes, this is not being dutiful towards them.

بَاب: الْجِهَادُ بِإِذْنِ الْأَبَوَيْنِ الْمُسْلِمَيْنِ

Chapter: Jihad with the permission of Muslim parents

HADITH 9

عَنْ عَبْدِ اللهِ بْنِ عَمْرٍو ﵄ قَالَ: قَالَ رَجُلٌ لِلنَّبِيِّ ﷺ أُجَاهِدُ؟ قَالَ: لَكَ أَبَوَانِ؟ قَالَ: نَعَمْ، قَالَ: فَفِيْهِمَا فَجَاهِدْ.

ʿAbdullāh ibn ʿAmr ﵄ narrates, 'A man said to the Prophet ﷺ, "Can I undertake jihad?" He [ﷺ] said, "Are your parents alive?" He replied, "Yes." He [ﷺ] said, 'Then exert yourself in their service." *Ṣaḥīḥ al-Bukhārī* (3004, 5972), *Ṣaḥīḥ Muslim* (2549).

HADITH 10

عَنْ عَبْدِ اللهِ بْنِ عَمْرٍو ﵄ قَالَ: جَاءَ رَجُلٌ إِلَى النَّبِيِّ ﷺ يُبَايِعُهُ عَلَى الْهِجْرَةِ، فَتَرَكَ أَبَوَيْهِ يَبْكِيَانِ؟ قَالَ: ارْجِعْ إِلَيْهِمَا فَأَضْحِكْهُمَا كَمَا أَبْكَيْتَهُمَا.

ʿAbdullāh ibn ʿAmr ﵄ narrates, 'A man came to the Prophet ﷺ to pledge allegiance to migrate and left his parents crying. He [ﷺ] said, "Return to them and make them laugh, just as you made them cry."' *Al-Adab al-Mufrad* (19), *Sunan Abī Dāwūd* (2528), *Sunan an-Nasa'ī* (4163), *Sunan Ibn Mājah* (2782)

Commentary: It is prohibited for a person to undertake jihad (fight in the path of Allah) if their parents refuse permission, provided they are Muslims and that jihad is a communal obligation. This is because obedience to parents is obligatory on every person and it, therefore, supersedes the communal obligation of jihad. However, if jihad becomes an obligation on every person, because of an enemy invasion or occupation, for example, then parental consent is not necessary and jihad will be obligatory.

بَاب: مَنْ بُسِطَ لَهُ فِي الرِّزْقِ بِصِلَةِ الرَّحِمِ وَأَعْظَمُ الصِّلَةِ صِلَةُ الوَالِدَيْنِ

Chapter: The person whose sustenance is expanded due to maintaining ties of kinship and the greatest family tie is the bond of parents

HADITH 11

عَنْ أَنَسِ بْنِ مَالِكٍ ﵁ أَنَّ رَسُوْلَ اللهِ ﷺ قَالَ: مَنْ أَحَبَّ أَنْ يُبْسَطَ لَهُ فِيْ رِزْقِهِ وَيُنْسَأَ لَهُ فِيْ أَثَرِهِ فَلْيَصِلْ رَحِمَه.

Anas ibn Mālik ﵁ narrates that Allah's Messenger ﷺ said, 'Whoever desires for his sustenance to be expanded and his life to be pro-longed should maintain his ties of kinship.'[1]

HADITH 12

عَنْ أَنَسِ بْنِ مَالِكٍ ﵁ قَالَ: قَالَ رَسُوْلُ اللهِ ﷺ: مَنْ أَحَبَّ أَن يُمَدَّ لَهُ فِيْ عُمرِهِ وَيُزَادَ لَهُ فِيْ رِزْقِهِ فَلْيَبَرَّ وَالِدَيْهِ.

Anas ibn Mālik ﵁ narrates, 'The Messenger of Allah ﷺ said, "Whoever desires for his life to be lengthened and sustenance to be increased should be dutiful to his parents."'[2]

1 *Ṣaḥīḥ al-Bukhārī* (2067, 5986), *Al-Adab al-Mufrad* (56), *Ṣaḥīḥ Muslim* (2557).

2 *Musnad Aḥmad* (13401, 13811), *Ḥilyat al-Awliyā'* (3:107), *Shu'ab al-Īmān* (7471).

Commentary: Scholars have discussed the meaning of life being prolonged or age being extended. Some scholars prefer the literal meaning and suggest that this is in accordance with the knowledge of the angels, otherwise Allah Almighty knows the age of all humans. Shaykh al-Islam Ibn Taymiyyah (d. 728/1328) is inclined to this view (*Majmūʿ al-Fatāwā* (8:517, 14:490). Other scholars suggest that this is a metaphorical reference to blessing in a person's life and the ability to do many more good deeds in a shorter period of time, good health, pious children who will supplicate for their parents, or a continuation of their legacy and praise among people after their demise.[1] Imam Nawawī (d. 676/1277), in his commentary of *Ṣaḥīḥ Muslim* (16:114), gives preference to the non-literal interpretation.

---

1 *Sharḥ Ibn Baṭṭāl ʿalā Ṣaḥīḥ al-Bukhārī*, 6:206; *Kashf al-Mushkil*, 3:185.

بَاب: دَعْوَةِ الْوَالِدَيْنِ

Chapter: The supplication of parents

HADITH 13

عَنْ أَبِي هُرَيْرَةَ ﷺ يَقُوْلُ: قَالَ رَسُوْلُ اللهِ ﷺ: ثَلاَثُ دَعَوَاتٍ مُسْتَجَابَاتٌ لَهُنَّ، لاَ شَكَّ فِيْهِنَّ: دَعْوَةُ الْمَظْلُومِ، وَدَعْوَةُ الْمُسَافِرِ، وَدَعْوَةُ الْوَالِدِ عَلَى وَلَدِهِ.

Abū Hurayrah ﷺ narrates, 'The Messenger of Allah ﷺ said, "Three supplications are answered without any doubt: the supplication of the oppressed, the supplication of the traveller, and the supplication of the parent against their child."' *Al-Adab al-Mufrad* (32), *Sunan Abī Dāwūd* (1536), *Jāmiʿ at-Tirmidhī* (1905).

Commentary: The story of Jurayj is a perfect illustration of this and should serve as a reminder for parents to exercise restraint when supplicating against their children and for children to avoid causing such parental supplications. Imam Bukhārī has transmitted the story of Jurayj in *Al-Adab al-Mufrad* in detail. Refer to Appendix 2 for the full narration. An abridged version of the story has also been transmitted in *Ṣaḥīḥ al-Bukhārī*. Jurayj was an extremely pious person who was able to make a newborn baby speak miraculously through the power of Almighty Allah. However, Jurayj was not spared from the supplication of his mother against him.

The reference to the 'oppressed' in the hadith includes all forms of oppression: physical, psychological, emotional, verbal or otherwise.

بَاب: عُقُوْقِ الْوَالِدَيْنِ يُحْبِطُ الْعَمَل

Chapter: Disobedience of parents nullifies actions

HADITH 14

عَنْ أَبِيْ أَمَامَةَ الْبَاهِلِيِّ ﵁ عَنْ رَسُوْلِ اللهِ ﷺ قَالَ: ثَلاثَةٌ لَا يَقْبَلُ اللهُ لَهُمْ صَرْفًا وَلاَ عَدْلاً: عَاقٌّ، وَمَنَّانٌ، وَمُكَذِّبٌ بِالْقَدَرِ.

Abū Umāmah al-Bāhilī ﵁ narrates from the Messenger of Allah ﷺ, who said, 'There are three [people] from whom Allah will not accept any obligatory deed, nor any supererogatory deed: the disobeyer [of his parents], one who is boastful [of favours on others] and the rejector of predestination.' [1]

Commentary: This chapter is a warning against the disobedience of parents, as it is a sin that resembles disbelief, although disobedience itself is not disbelief. Scholars have outlined various meanings of the Arabic terms '*ṣarf*' and '*ʿadl*,' with Imam Khaṭṭābī (d. 383/993) suggesting that they mean obligatory (*farḍ*) and supererogatory (*nafl*) deeds respectively, as in the translation above (*Maʿālim as-Sunan* (4:22)). Some scholars suggest '*ṣarf*' refers to repentance and '*ʿadl*' refers to compensation. There are also other views.[2]

1 *Al-Muʿjam al-Kabīr* (7547); *Musnad ash-Shāmiyyīn* (1431); *Kitāb al-Qaḍā' wa'l-Qadar* (380).

2 *Sharḥ Ibn Baṭṭāl ʿalā Ṣaḥīḥ al-Bukhārī*, 4:541; *Fatḥ al-Bārī*, 1:144.

بَاب: جَزَاءِ الْوَالِدَيْنِ

Chapter: Repaying parents

HADITH 15

عَنْ أَبِيْ هُرَيْرَةَ ﷺ عَنِ النَّبِيِّ ﷺ قَالَ: لاَ يَجْزِيْ وَلَدٌ وَالِدَيْهِ إِلاَّ أَنْ يَجِدَهُ مَمْلُوْكًا فَيَشْتَرِيَهُ فَيُعْتِقَهُ.

Abū Hurayrah ﷺ narrates from the Prophet ﷺ, who said, 'A child cannot repay his parents unless he finds one of them as a slave, then purchases him and sets him free.'[1]

Commentary: Imam Khaṭṭābī explains in *Maʿālim as-Sunan* (4:150) that as soon as a child purchases a slave father, the father will automatically be free. This is the view of the majority of scholars, with the exception of Imam Dāwūd aẓ-Ẓāhirī (d. 270/884) (*Kashf al-Mushkil* (3:566)). Imam Khaṭṭābī adds that the reason for the hadith regarding this action as repayment is that freedom from slavery is the best favour one can bestow upon a human being. Imam Ibn Hubayrah al-Wazīr (d. 560/1165) suggests in *Ifṣāḥ* (8:112) that this is a rare occurrence and therefore in normal circumstances, it is beyond comprehension for children to truly repay their parents.

1 *Al-Adab Al-Mufrad* (10), *Ṣaḥīḥ Muslim* (1510), *At-Targhīb wa't-Tarhīb* (452).

بَاب: عُقُوْقِ الْوَالِدَيْنِ مِنَ الْكَبَائِرِ

Chapter: Disobedience of parents is from the major sins

HADITH 16

عَنْ أَبِيْ بَكْرَةَ ﷺ قَالَ: قَالَ النَّبِيُّ ﷺ: أَلَا أُنَبِّئُكُمْ بِأَكْبَرِ الْكَبَائِرِ؟ ثَلَاثًا، قَالُوْا: بَلَى يَا رَسُوْلَ اللهِ، قَالَ: الإِشْرَاكُ بِاللهِ وَعُقُوْقُ الْوَالِدَيْنِ، وَجَلَسَ وَكَانَ مُتَّكِئًا، فَقَالَ: وَقَوْلُ الزُّوْرِ، فَمَا زَالَ يُكَرِّرُهَا حَتَّى قُلْنَا: لَيْتَهُ سَكَتَ.

Abū Bakrah ﷺ narrates, 'The Prophet ﷺ said thrice, "Shall I not inform you of the gravest of the major sins?' They replied, "Certainly, O Messenger of Allah." He [ﷺ] said, "Associating partners with Allah and disobeying parents," and he [ﷺ] sat up, as he had been reclining, and said, "and false testimony." He continued to repeat it until we said [to ourselves], "We hope he becomes silent."' *Ṣaḥīḥ al-Bukhārī* (5976), *Al-Adab al-Mufrad* (15), *Ṣaḥīḥ Muslim* (87).

Commentary: This narration is evidence that there are three categories of sins: minor, major and the gravest of major sins. (For a detailed analysis of the categories of sins and their definitions, refer to Imam Nawawī's commentary on *Ṣaḥīḥ Muslim* (2:84))

Imam Ibn al-Jawzī (d. 597/1201) highlights in *Kashf al-Mushkil* (2:13) that the list in this hadith is not comprehensive, because murder and fornication are also examples of the gravest major sins. The

Prophet ﷺ made reference to these specific sins here, as they were more widespread in society, or because he feared they were more likely to be committed.

The narration also affirms the permissibility for a scholar to sit in a reclining position, although this was not the general practice of the Prophet ﷺ, a point deduced by Imam Muhallab (d. 435/1044) (*Sharḥ Ibn Baṭṭāl ʿalā Ṣaḥīḥ al-Bukhārī* (9:55)).

بَاب: صَغَارِ مَنْ أَدْرَكَ وَالِدَيْهِ فَلَمْ يَدْخُلِ الْجَنَّةَ

Chapter: The deplorable nature of someone who finds his parents [in old age] and does not enter Paradise [through dutifulness to them]

HADITH 17

عَنْ أَبِي هُرَيْرَةَ ﷺ عَنِ النَّبِيِّ ﷺ قَالَ: رَغِمَ أَنْفُهُ، رَغِمَ أَنْفُهُ، رَغِمَ أَنْفُهُ، قَالُوْا: يَا رَسُولَ اللهِ، مَنْ؟ قَالَ: مَنْ أَدْرَكَ وَالِدَيْهِ عِنْدَ الْكِبَرِ أَوْ أَحَدَهُمَا فَدَخَلَ النَّارَ.

Abū Hurayrah ﷺ narrates from the Prophet ﷺ, who said, 'Disgraced! Disgraced! Disgraced!' They said, 'O Messenger of Allah, who?' He said, 'The person who finds his parents, or one of them, in old age, yet he enters the fire.' *Al-Adab al-Mufrad* (21), *Ṣaḥīḥ Muslim* (2551).

HADITH 18

عَنْ أَبِي هُرَيْرَةَ ﷺ عَنِ النَّبِيِّ ﷺ قَالَ: رَغِمَ أَنْفُهُ، رَغِمَ أَنْفُهُ، رَغِمَ أَنْفُهُ، ثَلَاثَ مَرَّاتٍ، مَنْ أَدْرَكَ وَالِدَيْهِ أَوْ أَحَدَهُمَا عِنْدَ الْكِبَرِ فَيَدْخُلُ النَّارَ أَوْ: لَمْ يَدْخُلِ الْجَنَّةَ.

Abū Hurayrah ﷺ narrates from the Prophet ﷺ, who said, 'Disgraced! Disgraced! Disgraced!' three times. 'The person who finds his parents, or one of them, in old age, yet he enters the fire (or: he does not enter Paradise).' *Ṣaḥīḥ Muslim* (2551), *Musnad Aḥmad* (8557).

HADITH 19

عَنْ أَبِيْ هُرَيْرَةَ ﵁ عَنِ النَّبِيِّ ﷺ قَالَ: رَغِمَ أَنْفُ رَجُلٍ ذُكِرْتُ عِنْدَهُ فَلَمْ يُصَلِّ عَلَيَّ، رَغِمَ أَنْفُ رَجُلٍ أَدْرَكَ أَبَوَيْهِ عِنْدَ الْكِبَرِ أَوْ أَحَدَهُمَا فَلَمْ يُدْخِلاَهُ الْجَنَّةَ، وَرَغِمَ أَنْفُ رَجُلٍ دَخَلَ عَلَيْهِ رَمَضَانُ ثُمَّ انْسَلَخَ قَبْلَ أَنْ يُغْفَرَ لَهُ.

Abū Hurayrah ﵁ narrates from the Prophet ﷺ, who said, 'Disgraced is the person who does not send salutations upon me when I am mentioned in his presence. Disgraced is the person who finds his parents, or one of them, in old age and they are not a means of his entry into Paradise. Disgraced is the person on whom Ramaḍān enters and then ends before he is forgiven.'[1]

HADITH 20

عَنْ كَعْبِ بْنِ عُجْرَةَ ﵁ قَالَ: قَالَ النَّبِيُّ ﷺ: أَحْضِرُوا الْمِنْبَرَ، فَلَمَّا خَرَجَ فَرَقِيَ الْمِنْبَرَ فَرَقِيَ اَوَّلَ دَرَجَةٍ مِنْهُ قَالَ: آمِين، ثُمَّ رَقِيَ فِي الثَّانِيَةِ فَقَالَ: آمِيْن، ثُمَّ لَمَّا رَقِيَ الثَّالِثَةَ قَالَ: آمِيْن، فَلَمَّا فَرَغَ وَنَزَلَ عَنِ الْمِنْبَرِ قُلْنَا: يَا رَسُوْلَ اللهِ، لَقَدْ سَمِعْنَا مِنْكَ الْيَوْمَ شَيْئًا مَا كُنَّا نَسْمَعُهُ مِنْكَ، قَالَ: وَسَمِعْتُمُوْهُ؟ قُلْنَا: نَعَمْ، قَالَ: إِنَّ جِبْرِيْلَ ﵇ اعْتَرَضَ، قَالَ: بَعُدَ مَنْ أَدْرَكَ رَمَضَانَ فَلَمْ يُغْفَرْ لَهُ، فَقُلْتُ: آمِين، فَلَمَّا رَقِيتُ الثَّانِيَةَ قَالَ: بَعُدَ

1 *Ṣaḥīḥ Ibn Ḥibbān* (908); *Musnad Aḥmad* (7541); *Jāmiʿ at-Tirmidhī* (3545); *Al-Mustadrak ʿalā aṣ-Ṣaḥīḥayn*, 1:549.

مَنْ ذُكِرْتَ عِنْدَهُ فَلَمْ يُصَلِّ عَلَيْكَ، فَقُلْتُ: آمِينَ، فَلَمَّا رَقِيتُ الثَّالِثَةَ قَالَ: بَعُدَ مَنْ أَدْرَكَ عِنْدَهُ أَبَوَاهُ الْكِبَرَ أَوْ أَحَدُهُمَا فَلَمْ يُدْخِلَاهُ الْجَنَّةَ، قُلْتُ: آمِينَ.

Kaʿb ibn ʿUjrah ؓ narrates that the Prophet ﷺ said, 'Bring the pulpit.' Then when he [ﷺ] emerged and ascended the pulpit, he ascended the first step and said, '*Āmīn*.' Then he ascended the second [step] and said, '*Āmīn*.' Then when he ascended the third [step] he said, '*Āmīn*.' Then when he had finished and descended the pulpit, we said, 'O Messenger of Allah, we have indeed heard something from you today which we have not heard before. He asked, 'And you heard it?' We replied, 'Yes.' He said, 'Indeed, Jibrīl ؑ appeared and said, "Distant [from the mercy of Allah] is he who reaches Ramaḍān and is not forgiven," so I said, "*Āmīn*." Then when I ascended the second [step], he said, "Distant is he who does not send salutations upon you when you are mentioned in his presence," so I said, "*Āmīn*." Then when I ascended the third, he said, "Distant is he who finds his parents, or one of them, in old age and they are not a means of his entry into Paradise," so I said, "*Āmīn*."[1]

Commentary: The purpose of this chapter and the narrations is clear: Serving one's elderly parents and fulfilling their needs is an easy means of entry into Paradise. Thus, if a person finds both his parents, or one of them, in old age, and despite this does not enter Paradise because of his failure to serve them, this is a sign of disgrace and humiliation. Qāḍī ʿIyāḍ (d. 554/1149) suggests in *Ikmāl al-Muʿlim* (8:14) that the apparent wording of the narrations implies that being dutiful to elderly parents itself expiates major sins.

---

1 *At-Tārīkh al-Kabīr*, 7:220; *Al-Muʿjam al-Kabīr* (15647), *Al-Mustadrak ʿalā aṣ-Ṣaḥīḥayn*, 4:180; *Shuʿab al-Īmān* (1471).

بَاب: نَظْرِ الْوَالِدِ لِوَلَدِهِ

Chapter: The parent's gaze upon their child

HADITH 21

عَنِ ابْنِ عَبَّاسٍ ﷺ قَالَ: قَالَ النَّبِيُّ ﷺ: إِذَا نَظَرَ الْوَالِدُ إِلَى وَلَدِهِ فَسَرَّهُ كَانَ لِلْوَلَدِ عِتْقُ نَسَمَةٍ.

Ibn ʿAbbās ﷺ narrates, 'The Prophet ﷺ said, "When a parent gazes upon their child and he makes them happy, the child gains [the reward of] freeing a soul."' *Al-Muʿjam al-Kabīr* (11634), *Al-Muʿjam al-Awsaṭ* (8646).

Commentary: ʿAllāmah Munāwī (d. 1031/1622) explains in *Fayḍ al-Qadīr* (1:448) that this reward is earned by the child because he attains his parent's pleasure through obedience, kindness and being dutiful towards them. Although the chain of this narration contains weakness, Ḥāfiẓ Haythamī (d. 807/1405) classified the narration as '*ḥasan*' (good) in *Majmaʿ az-Zawāʾid* (8:286).

The reward of freeing a soul can be ascertained from the narration transmitted in *Ṣaḥīḥ al-Bukhārī* (6715) wherein the Prophet ﷺ said, 'Whoever frees a Muslim slave, Allah will free from the Fire every part of his body in lieu of him freeing the corresponding parts of the slave's body, even his private parts in lieu of freeing the slave's private parts.'

بَاب: بِرِّ مَنْ كَانَ يَصِلُهُ أَبُوهُ

Chapter: Kindness to someone with whom one's father maintained ties

HADITH 22

عَنِ ابْنِ عُمَرَ ﵄ عَنْ رَسُوْلِ اللهِ ﷺ قَالَ: إِنَّ أَبَرَّ الْبِرِّ أَنْ يَصِلَ الرَّجُلُ أَهْلَ وُدِّ أَبِيْهِ.

Ibn ʿUmar ﵄ narrates from the Messenger of Allah ﷺ, who said, 'Indeed, the strongest form of dutifulness is for a person to maintain ties with the loved ones of his father.'[1]

Commentary: The narration in *Ṣaḥīḥ Muslim* (2552) has the following addition: 'after he is absent,' referring to the father's death, although it could also include his absence during his lifetime, for example during travels (*Mirqāt al-Mafātīḥ* (7:3083)). The Prophet ﷺ mentioned this specifically because a person's friends and associates are quickly forgotten after a person's demise.

The term 'loved ones' (*ahl wudd*) used in the narration includes the father's friends, whether they are relatives or not. Imam Nawawī adds in his commentary on *Ṣaḥīḥ Muslim* (16:110) that this advice also applies to the friends of the mother, grandparents, teachers, husband and wife, as demonstrated by the fact that the Prophet ﷺ would honour the friends of Khadījah ﵂ after her demise.

Shaykh al-Islam Ibn Taymiyyah mentions that, in addition to

1 *Al-Adab al-Mufrad* (41), *Ṣaḥīḥ Muslim* (2552), *Musnad Aḥmad* (5721), *Ṣaḥīḥ Ibn Ḥibbān* (430).

maintaining ties with a father's friends, a person should also supplicate for his parents and seek forgiveness for them after their demise, as mentioned in hadiths (*Majmūʿ al-Fatāwā* (1:222)).

SECTION 2

Maintaining Ties of Kinship

أَبْوَابُ صِلَةِ الرَّحِمِ

The Chapters on Maintaining the Ties of Kinship

Commentary: The purpose of the chapters within this section is to highlight that the narrations on the subject of maintaining ties of kinship include maintaining ties with parents, as they are the closest in relation to a person. Most of the narrations and chapters from this point onwards pertain to maintaining ties of kinship generally. However, there are a few chapters and narrations that are specific to parents.

The saint (*walī*) and hadith scholar Imam Ibn Abī Jamrah (d. 699/1296) explains that ties of kinship are maintained through financial support, providing support when in need, removing harm, being cheerful and pleasant and supplicating for them. He adds that the crux of maintaining ties is to benefit them with all forms of good and remove all forms of evil and harm from them as far as possible (*Fatḥ al-Bārī* (10:418)).

بَاب: إِثْمِ قَاطِعِ الرَّحِمِ

Chapter: The sin of someone who severs ties of kinship

HADITH 23

عَنْ أَبِي هُرَيْرَةَ ﷺ عَنِ النَّبِيِّ ﷺ قَالَ: إِنَّ اللهَ خَلَقَ الرَّحِمَ شُجْنَةً، أَمَا تَرْضَيْنَ أَنْ أُدْخِلَ الْجَنَّةَ مَنْ وَصَلَكِ وَأُدْخِلَ النَّارَ مَنْ قَطَعَكِ.

Abū Hurayrah ﷺ narrates from the Prophet ﷺ, who said, 'Indeed, Allah has created the ties of kinship as [interweaving] branches. [Allah says to the ties of kinship:] "Are you not pleased that I enter into Paradise the one who maintains you, and I enter into the Fire the one who severs you?"'[1]

HADITH 24

عَنْ جُبَيْرِ بْنِ مُطْعِمٍ ﷺ أَنَّهُ سَمِعَ النَّبِيَّ ﷺ يَقُوْلُ: لَا يَدْخُلُ الْجَنَّةَ قَاطِعٌ.

Jubayr ibn Muṭʿim ﷺ narrates that he heard the Prophet ﷺ say, 'A person who severs ties will not enter Paradise.' *Al-Adab al-Mufrad* (64), *Musnad Aḥmad* (16763).

Commentary: Imam Bukhārī has clarified after three chapters that entry into hellfire shall not be perpetual for a Muslim. ʿAllāmah Ibn

1 This narration with these words was not found in other works. However, there are hadiths with similar wordings.

Baṭṭāl explains in *Sharḥ Ṣaḥīḥ al-Bukhārī* (9:203) that the position of those who adhere to the Sunnah and the Community who follow it (*ahl as-Sunnah wal-Jamāʿah*) is that a Muslim's entry into hellfire is at the discretion of Almighty Allah, who may forgive and grant entry into Paradise or punish temporarily before entering the perpetrator into Paradise. Qāḍī ʿIyāḍ adds in *Ikmāl al-Muʿlim* (8:20) that if this narration is to be taken literally, then it refers to a person who regards it lawful to sever ties, as this is disbelief.

بَاب: مَنْ بُوْرِكَ لَهُ فِيْ رِزْقِهِ لِصِلَتِهِ رَحِمَهُ

Chapter: The person who is blessed in his sustenance due to maintaining his ties of kinship

HADITH 25

عَنْ أَنَسٍ ﷺ أَنَّ رَسُوْلَ اللهِ ﷺ قَالَ: مَنْ أَحَبَّ أَنْ يُبْسَطَ لَهُ فِيْ رِزْقِهِ وَيُنْسَأَ لَهُ فِيْ أَثَرِهِ فَلْيَصِلْ رَحِمَهُ.

Anas ﷺ narrates that Allah's Messenger ﷺ said, 'Whoever desires for his sustenance to be expanded and his life to be lengthened should maintain his ties of kinship.' *Al-Adab al-Mufrad* (56), *Musnad al-Bazzār* (6316).

Commentary: The commentary of this narration has already been outlined. Imam Bukhārī has repeated this narration here to affirm that the benefits mentioned therein are not restricted to maintaining good relations with parents.

بَاب: يَصِلُ اللهُ تَعَالَى بِفَضْلِهِ مَنْ وَصَلَ رَحِمَهُ

Chapter: Allah the Exalted maintains ties through His grace with the person who maintains his ties of kinship

HADITH 26

عَنْ أَبِيْ هُرَيْرَةَ ﷺ يُحَدِّثُ عَنْ رَسُوْلِ اللهِ ﷺ قَالَ: إِنَّ الرَّحِمَ شُجْنَةٌ [مِنَ الرَّحْمَنِ]، تَقُوْلُ: يَا رَبِّ، إِنِّي ظُلِمْتُ، إِنِّي قُطِعْتُ، يَا رَبِّ، يَا رَبِّ، يَا رَبِّ، فَيُجِيبُهَا: أَلاَ تَرْضَيْنَ أَنْ أَقْطَعَ مَنْ قَطَعَكِ وَأَصِلَ مَنْ وَصَلَكِ؟

Abū Hurayrah ﷺ narrates that the Messenger of Allah ﷺ said, 'Indeed, *raḥim* (ties of kinship) is a branch [derived from *Raḥmān* (the All-Merciful)]. It says, "O my Lord! I have been wronged! O, My Lord! I have been severed! O My Lord! O My Lord! O My Lord!" He answers it, "Are you not pleased that I sever the one who severs you, and I maintain the one who maintains you?"'[1]

Commentary: Imam Ibn al-Jawzī explains in *Kashf al-Mushkil* (3:405) that the phrase, '*raḥim* is derived from *Raḥmān*,' could signify the close connection between ties of kinship and Almighty Allah. Alternatively, it could be a reference to the fact that both share the same semantic origin in Arabic, thus denoting the importance of *raḥim*. Imam Ibn Jarīr aṭ-Ṭabarī (d. 310/923) explains that with regard to a person who maintains ties of kinship, Almighty Allah will have mercy on him

1 *Al-Adab al-Mufrad* (65), *At-Tārīkh al-Kabīr*, 1:168, *Musnad Aḥmad* (9871), *Al-Mustadrak ʿalā aṣ-Ṣaḥīḥayn*, 4:179.

through His grace, either in this world or in the Hereafter (*Sharḥ Ibn Baṭṭāl ʿalā Ṣaḥīḥ al-Bukhārī* (9:205)). As for a person who severs ties of kinship, Allah will deprive him of His mercy and grace.

بَاب: لَا يَدْخُلُ الْمُسْلِمُ إِذَا كَانَ عَاقًّا لِوَالِدَيْهِ الْجَنَّةَ اِبْتِدَاءً

Chapter: The Muslim who disobeys his parents will not enter Paradise initially

HADITH 27

عَنْ أَبِي الدَّرْدَاءِ ﵁ عَنِ النَّبِيِّ ﷺ قَالَ: لَا يَدْخُلُ الْجَنَّةَ عَاقٌّ وَلَا مُدْمِنُ خَمْرٍ وَلَا مُكَذِّبٌ بِالْقَدَرِ.

Abū ad-Dardā' ﵁ narrates from the Prophet ﷺ, who said, 'The disobeyer [of parents] will not enter Paradise, nor the alcoholic, nor someone who denies divine decree.' *Musnad Aḥmad* (27484), *Musnad al-Bazzār* (4106), *Musnad ash-Shāmiyyīn* (2212), *At-Targhīb wa't-Tarhīb* (463, 2205).

Commentary: Imam Bukhārī is highlighting the punishment of the one who disobeys his parents, but at the same time affirming the position of the *ahl as-Sunnah wa'l-Jamāʿah* that all Muslims will eventually enter Paradise, as previously mentioned.

بَاب: لَيْسَ الْوَاصِلُ بِالْمُكَافِئِ

Chapter: The person who maintains ties of kinship is not someone who [merely] reciprocates

HADITH 28

عَنْ عَبْدِ اللهِ بْنِ عَمْرٍو ﵄ قَالَ: قَالَ رَسُوْلُ اللهِ ﷺ: لَيْسَ الْوَاصِلُ بِالْمُكَافِئِ، وَلَكِنِ الْوَاصِلُ الَّذِيْ تُقْطَعُ رَحِمُهُ فَيَصِلُهَا.

ʿAbdullāh ibn ʿAmr ﵄ narrates, 'The Messenger of Allah ﷺ said, "The person who maintains ties of kinship is not someone who [merely] reciprocates; rather, the person who maintains ties of kinship is he who maintains them when they are severed."' *Ṣaḥīḥ al-Bukhārī* (5991), *Al-Adab al-Mufrad* (68).

Commentary: Reciprocating good is commendable and a means of reward. However, the Prophet ﷺ explains that the true and complete *wāṣil* (the person who maintains ties of kinship) is he who goes a step further and mends severed ties, as this is the more difficult task (*Fatḥ al-Bārī* (10:423)). Imam Ibn al-Jawzī draws an analogy between someone who reciprocates favours and someone repaying a debt.[1]

1 *Kashf al-Mushkil*, 4:120.

بَاب: مَنْ وَصَلَ رحِمَهُ وَصَلَهُ اللهُ تَعَالَى

Chapter: Whoever maintains his ties of kinship, Allah the Exalted maintains ties with him

HADITH 29

عَنْ عَائِشَةَ زَوْجِ النَّبِيِّ ﵂ عَنِ النَّبِيِّ ﷺ قَالَ: الرَّحِمُ شُجْنَةٌ، فَمَنْ وَصَلَهَا وَصَلْتُهُ، وَمَنْ قَطَعَهَا قَطَعْتُهُ.

ʿĀ'ishah, the wife of the Prophet, ﵂ narrates from the Prophet ﷺ, who said, '*Raḥim* (ties of kinship) is a branch [as it is derived from *Raḥmān*]. [Allah Almighty said:] Therefore, whoever maintains it, I will keep good relations with him, and whoever severs it, I will sever him.' *Ṣaḥīḥ al-Bukhārī* (5989), *Al-Adab al-Mufrad* (55).

Commentary: See Hadiths 24 and 26.

بَاب: لا تَنْزِلُ الرَّحْمَةُ عَلَى قَوْمٍ فِيْهِمْ قَاطِعُ رَحِمٍ

Chapter: Mercy does not descend upon a people who have among them a person who severs the ties of kinship

HADITH 30

عَنْ عَبْدِ اللهِ بْنِ أَبِيْ أَوْفَى ﷺ عَنِ النَّبِيِّ ﷺ قَالَ: إِنَّ الرَّحْمَةَ لاَ تَنْزِلُ عَلَى قَوْمٍ فِيهِمْ قَاطِعُ رَحِمٍ.

ʿAbdullāh ibn Abī Awfā ﷺ narrates from the Prophet ﷺ, who said, 'Indeed, mercy does not descend upon a people who have among them a person who severs ties of kinship.'[1]

Commentary: ʿAllāmah Tūrībishtī (d. ca. 660/1261) writes in the commentary on *Maṣābīḥ as-Sunnah* (3:1069), 'It is possible that 'people' refers to those who support him in severing ties and do not disapprove of it. It is possible that 'mercy' refers to rain; that is, they are deprived of rain due to the misfortune of the person who severs ties of kinship.' ʿAllāmah Munāwī adds in *Fayḍ al-Qadīr* (2:340) that this narration proves that severing ties of kinship is a major sin.

1 Ibid. (63); *At-Tārīkh al-Kabīr*, 4:14; *Zuhd Wakīʿ* (405); *Al-Maʿrifah wa't-Tārīkh*, 1:109.

بَاب: إِثْمِ الْقَاطِعِ

Chapter: The sin of the person who severs the ties of kinship

HADITH 31

عَنْ جُبَيْرِ بْنِ مُطْعِمٍ رضي الله عنه أَنَّهُ سَمِعَ رَسُوْلَ اللهِ ﷺ يَقُوْلُ: لاَ يَدْخُلُ الْجَنَّةَ قَاطِعٌ.

Jubayr ibn Muṭ'im ﷺ narrates that he heard the Prophet ﷺ say, 'The person who severs the ties of kinship will not enter Paradise.'[1]

HADITH 32

عَنْ أَبِيْ هُرَيْرَةَ رضي الله عنه عَنِ النَّبِيِّ ﷺ قَالَ: إِنَّ الرَّحِمَ شُجْنَةٌ تَقُوْلُ: يَا رَبِّ إِنِّي قُطِعْتُ، يَا رَبِّ ظُلِمْتُ، يَا رَبِّ يَا رَبِّ يَا رَبِّ، فَيُجِيْبُهَا: أَلاَ تَرْضَيْنَ أَنْ أَقْطَعَ مَنْ قَطَعَكِ وَأَصِلَ مَنْ وَصَلَكِ.

Abū Hurayrah ﷺ narrates that the Prophet ﷺ said, 'Indeed, *raḥim* (ties of kinship) is a branch [as it is derived from *Raḥmān* (All-Merciful)]. It says, "O My Lord! Verily, I have been severed! O, my Lord! I have been wronged! O My Lord! O My Lord! O My Lord!" So, He answers them, "Are you not pleased that I sever

1 *Ṣaḥīḥ al-Bukhārī* (5984), *Al-Adab Al-Mufrad* (63), *Shu'ab al-Īmān* (7952), *Mu'jam aṭ-Ṭabarānī al-Kabīr* (1510).

the one who severs you and I maintain the one who maintains you?"'[1]

Commentary: *See Hadith 26.*

1 *Al-Adab al-Mufrad* (65), *At-Tārīkh al-Kabīr*, 1:168, *Musnad Aḥmad* (9871), *Al-Mustadrak ʿalā aṣ-Ṣaḥīḥayn*, 4:179.

بَاب

Chapter

HADITH 33

قَالَ إِبْرَاهِيْمُ التَّيْمِيُّ ﷺ: مَثَّلْتُ نَفْسِيْ فِي الْجَنَّةِ، آكُلُ مِنْ طَعَامِهَا وَأَشْرَبُ مِنْ شَرَابِهَا، وَأُجَاوِرُ مَنْ فِيْهَا، وَأُصِيْبُ مَنْ أَشْتَهِيْ، ثُمَّ قُلْتُ: أَيْ نَفْسُ تَمَنَّيْ، قَالَتْ: أَتَمَنَّى أَنْ أَرْجِعَ إِلَى الدُّنْيَا فَأَزْدَادَ مِنَ الْعَمَلِ كَيْمَا أَزْدَادَ مِنَ الثَّوَابِ، ثُمَّ مَثَّلْتُ نَفْسِيْ فِي النَّارِ، آكُلُ مِنْ زَقُّوْمِهَا وَأَشْرَبُ مِن حَمِيْمِهَا [وَأُجَاوِرُ مَنْ فِيهَا]، ثُمَّ قُلْتُ: أَيْ نَفْسُ تَمَنَّيْ، قَالَتْ: أَتَمَنَّى أَنْ أَرْجِعَ إِلَى الدُّنْيَا فَأَتُوْبَ كَيْمَا أَنْجُوَ مِمَّا أَنَا فِيْه، فَقُلتُ لَهَا: أَيْ نَفْسِيْ فَأَنْتِ فِيْ أُمْنِيَّتِكِ فَاعْمَلِيْ.

Ibrahīm at-Taymī ﷺ said, 'I imagined myself in Paradise, eating from its delicacies, drinking from its beverages, cohabiting with its inhabitants and attaining what I desired. Then I said, "O soul, make a wish." It replied, "I wish to return to the world in order to increase in good deeds so that I increase in reward." Then I imagined myself in hellfire, eating from its cursed tree and drinking from its boiling water [and cohabiting with its inhabitants]. Then I said, "O soul, make a wish." It replied, "I wish to return to the world to repent so that I may be saved from the predicament I am in." Then I said to it, "O soul, you are [currently] in your dream, so do [good deeds, as you are still in the world]."'[1]

---

1 *Muḥāsabat an-Nafs* (10); *Ḥilyat al-Awliyā'*, 4:211; *Muntaẓam*, 6:305.

Commentary: Two points are worth noting here:

Firstly, it is Imam Bukhārī's habit to sometimes establish a chapter without a heading. Commentators of *Ṣaḥīḥ al-Bukhārī* have provided various generic and specific reasons for this whenever it occurs in his *Ṣaḥīḥ*. One of the generic reasons is that the narration in the chapter has a subtle connection with the previous chapter, which, at first glance, may not be obvious. In this context, Imam Bukhārī may be suggesting that the consequence of severing ties of kinship (as outlined in the previous chapter) is so severe that a person will wish to return to the world, because entry into the hellfire necessitates eating from its cursed tree and drinking from its boiling water (as mentioned in the narration of this chapter). An alternative way of considering this is that Imam Bukhārī is alerting the reader to remain engaged in good deeds whilst they are alive, particularly maintaining ties of kinship, as this will help them to achieve their dream of entry into Paradise or to attain a higher rank in Paradise.

Secondly, Imam Ibrāhīm ibn Yazīd at-Taymī (d. 92/710–1) is a famous *Tābiʿī* (Follower—someone who saw or accompanied a Companion of the Prophet ﷺ) saint (*walī*) and jurist. He transmits hadiths from several Companions and many leading scholars transmit hadiths from him. He passed away at a young age in prison, with some suggesting that he was killed by the leader Ḥajjāj ibn Yūsuf (d. 95/714) (*Siyar* (5:60); *Tahdhīb al-Kamāl* (2:232)).

بَاب: خَوْفِ الْمُؤْمِنِ مِنْ أَن يُحْبَطَ عَمَلُهُ وَهُوَ لَا يَشْعُرُ وَمِمَّا يُحْبِطُ الْعَمَلَ عُقُوْقُ الْوَالِدَيْنِ

Chapter: The believer's fear that his deeds will be nullified whilst he is unaware, and disobedience of parents is one of the nullifiers of deeds

HADITH 34

قَالَ إِبْرَاهِيْمُ التَّيْمِيُّ: مَا عَرَضْتُ قَوْلِيْ عَلَى عَمَلِيْ إِلَّا خَشِيْتُ أَنْ أَكُوْنَ مُكَذِّبًا.

Ibrahīm at-Taymī said, 'I do not compare my words to my deeds without fearing that I will be called a liar.'[1]

Commentary: Imam Ibrāhīm at-Taymī constantly worried about his actions being nullified on account of them not reflecting his speech. Imam Bukhārī is highlighting that a believer should always be fearful of his actions becoming nullified and that there are several causes for this; for example, lack of sincerity. Imam Bukhārī adds that disobedience of parents results in actions becoming nullified and one should, therefore, be fearful. A chapter with a similar theme appeared in Section 1 of this book, 'Chapter: Disobedience of parents nullifies actions.'

1 *At-Tārīkh al-Kabīr*, 1:335. This statement has also been cited in *Ṣaḥīḥ al-Bukhārī* (48) without the chain of transmission.

[بَاب]

[Chapter]

HADITH 35

عن جَابِرٍ ﷺ قَالَ: قَالَ النَّبِيُّ ﷺ: إِذَا جَاءَ أَحَدُكُمْ وَالْإِمَامُ يَخْطُبُ فَلْيَرْكَعْ رَكْعَتَيْنِ، قَالَ الْبُخَارِيُّ: وَبِهِ نَأْخُذُ.

Jābir [ibn ʿAbdillāh k] narrates, 'The Prophet ﷺ said, "When one of you comes [for the Friday Prayer] and the imam is delivering the sermon, then he should perform two units of prayer (*rakʿahs*)."' *Ṣaḥīḥ al-Bukhārī* (930), *Ṣaḥīḥ Muslim* (875). Bukhārī says, 'And this is [the practice] we adopt.'

Commentary: The relevance of this hadith to the subject of the book is not clear. Perhaps Imam Bukhārī is making a subtle reference to the issue of responding to the call of parents during prayer (*ṣalāh*) and, by extension, during the sermon. Listening to the sermon on Friday is obligatory. However, an exception to this is performing the two *rakʿahs* of *taḥiyyat al-masjid* (the prayer performed upon entry into the mosque), at least according to the Ḥanbalī and Shafiʿī schools of law. A similar exception applies to responding to the parent's call during the sermon, and also during prayer, as breaking the *ṣalāh* is generally prohibited.

Note: Performing two *rakʿahs* of *taḥiyyat al-masjid* prayer is an emphasised Sunnah according to all four schools of law, although some scholars say it is necessary (*wājib*). However, if a person enters the mosque whilst the imam is delivering the Friday sermon, he will not perform this prayer according to the Ḥanafī and Mālikī schools. According to the Ḥanbalī and Shāfiʿī schools, he will perform the prayer, a view shared by Imam Bukhārī. From an evidential perspective, this is the stronger position, which is why scholars like Shāh Waliyyullāh Dehlawī (d. 1176/1762) and ʿAllāmah Shabbīr Aḥmad ʿUthmānī (d. 1369/1949) are inclined to it. (*Ḥujjat Allah al-Bālighah*, 2:46; *Fatḥ al-Mulhim,* 4:346).

[بَاب]

[Chapter]

HADITH 36

قَالَ سُفْيَانُ بْنُ عُيَيْنَةَ: مَنْ لَا يَعْلَمُ وَيَعْلَمُ أَنَّهُ لَا يَعْلَمُ فَهُوَ عَالِمٌ.

Sufyān ibn ʿUyaynah said, 'Whoever does not know whilst he is aware that he does not know, then he is learned.'

Commentary: The relevance of this statement to the subject of the book is not entirely clear. Perhaps Imam Bukhārī is alluding to the fact that the lofty status of parents cannot be fully ascertained; however, the learned person is he who recognises this.

بَاب: لَا تَغْضَبْ وَلَا تُظْهِرْ غَضَبَكَ لِوَالِدَيْكَ

Chapter: Do not be angry, nor display your anger to your parents

HADITH 37

عَنْ أَبِيْ هُرَيْرَةَ رضي الله عنه قَالَ: جَاءَ رَجُلٌ إِلَى النَّبِيِّ ﷺ فَقَالَ: يَا رَسُوْلَ اللهِ أَوْصِنِيْ وَأَقْلِلْ لَعَلِّيْ أَعِيْهِ، قَالَ: لَا تَغْضَبْ، فَسَأَلَهُ مَرَّةً أَوْ مَرَّتَيْنِ كُلُّ ذٰلِكَ يَقُوْلُ: لَا تَغْضَبْ.

Abū Hurayrah ﷺ narrates, 'A man came to the Prophet ﷺ and said, "O Messenger of Allah, advise me and make it concise so that I may remember it." He [ﷺ] replied, "Do not become angry." The man asked him [the same] once or twice and he [ﷺ] replied each time, "Do not become angry."' *Ṣaḥīḥ al-Bukhārī* (6116), *Musnad Aḥmad* (10272).

HADITH 38

عَنْ أَبِيْ هُرَيْرَةَ رضي الله عنه قَالَ: قَالَ رَسُوْلُ اللهِ ﷺ: لَيْسَ الشَّدِيْدُ مَنْ غَلَبَ النَّاسَ وَلٰكِنَّ الشَّدِيْدَ مَنْ غَلَبَ نَفْسَهُ.

Abū Hurayrah ﷺ narrates, 'The Messenger of Allah ﷺ said, "The strong one is not he who overpowers people, rather the strong one is he who controls himself."'[1]

1 *Zuhd* (1302); *As-Sunan al-Kubrā li 'n-Nasa'ī* (10229); *Ṣaḥīḥ Ibn Ḥibbān* (717); *Sharḥ as-Sunnah li 'l-Baghawī* (3582).

Commentary: Imam Bukhārī uses these general narrations to highlight that displaying anger to parents is the worst form of anger. Imam Khaṭṭābī mentions in his commentary on *Ṣaḥīḥ al-Bukhārī* (3:2197) that the main cause of anger is pride and therefore the solution to anger is humility. Thus, the second narration of this chapter highlights that the true strength of a person is not determined by their physicality, but their inner or spiritual strength (for example, the ability to develop humility in place of anger), hence the correlation between both narrations.

بَاب: لاَ تُؤْذِ وَالِدَيْكَ بِكَلِمَة

Chapter: Do not hurt your parents [even] with a word

HADITH 39

عَنْ إِبْرَاهِيْمَ بْنِ عُمَرَ بْنِ كَيْسَانَ قَالَ: مَكَثَ ابْنُ أَبِي نَجِيحٍ ﷺ ثَلاَثِيْنَ سَنَةً لَا يَتَكَلَّمُ بِكَلِمَةٍ يُؤْذِي بِهَا جَلِيْسَهُ.

Ibrāhīm ibn ʿUmar ibn Kaysān said, 'Ibn Abī Najīḥ ﷺ spent thirty years without uttering any word which would harm his companion.' *At-Tārīkh al-Awsaṭ* (3:354).

Commentary: In the previous chapter, Imam Bukhārī warned against showing anger towards one's parents. Here he mentions that a person should not even utter a single word that would hurt them, let alone display anger towards them. As Almighty Allah says in the Qur'an:

﴿إِمَّا يَبْلُغَنَّ عِندَكَ الْكِبَرَ أَحَدُهُمَا أَوْ كِلَاهُمَا فَلَا تَقُل لَّهُمَا أُفٍّ﴾

If either of them, or both of them, reach old age with you, do not [even] say to them, 'Uff!' [i.e. a word or expression of the slightest disapproval] . . . Qur'an (17:23)

This narration transmitted by Imam Bukhārī is general and therefore applies to everyone, including parents.

بَاب: يَسْلَمُ النَاسُ مِنْ شَرِّ المُسلِمِ وَلاَ سِيَّماَ إِذَا كَانَا وَالِدَاهُ

Chapter: People should be safe from the wrong of a Muslim, especially if they are his parents

HADITH 40

عَنْ ابْنِ عُيَيْنَةَ: أَتَدْرُوْنَ مَا السَّلَامُ؟ السَّلَامُ أَنْتَ آمِنٌ مِنِّيْ أَنْتَ سَالِمٌ مِنِّي.

Ibn ʿUyaynah said, 'Do you know what '*salām*' is? '*Salām*' is that you are safe from me, you are secure from me.'

Commentary: The term '*salām*' is used by Muslims regularly when greeting one another, during prayer (*ṣalāh*) and supplications. The reason Imam Bukhārī has transmitted this narration here is to explain its meaning, thus emphasising that people in general, and parents in particular, should feel safe and secure from any harm or wrong of their children.

HADITH 41

سَمِعْتُ أَبَا عَبْدِ اللهِ المُسْنَدِيَّ يَقُوْلُ: جَاءَ سَلْمُ بْنُ سَالِمٍ إِلَى ابْنِ عُيَيْنَةَ ﵀ فَجَعَلَ يُسْمِعُهُ يَقُوْلُ: فَعَلْتُ كَذَا وَفَعَلْتُ كَذَا، قَالَ: فَنَظَرَ إِلَيْهِ ابْنُ عُيَيْنَةَ فَقَالَ: أَشْفَانِيْ مِنْكَ عَقْلُكَ، قَالَ اللهُ : ﴿وَأَعْرِضْ عَنِ الْجَاهِلِيْنَ﴾.

Abū ʿAbdillāh al-Musnadī narrates, 'Salm ibn Sālim came to Ibn ʿUyaynah ﵀ and began informing him, "I have done this and that." Ibn ʿUyaynah looked at him and said, "Your intellect has satisfied my view regarding you. Allah ﷻ says, *'And turn away from the ignorant.'*"' Qur'an (7:199)

Commentary: The context of this statement by Imam Sufyān ibn ʿUyaynah (d. 198/814) is that Salm ibn Sālim al-Balkhī (d. 194/810) was an extreme murji'ite who would invite others to his misguided beliefs. He has been classified as weak by hadith specialists. ʿAbdullāh ibn al-Mubārak (d. 181/797) deemed him a liar.[1] Perhaps Imam Bukhāri's rationale for transmitting this narration in this chapter is that a person should avoid harming others intellectually in matters pertaining to creed and beliefs, just as physical and verbal harm is to be avoided.

1 For his biographical entry, see: *Aṭ-Ṭabaqāt al-Kubrā*, 7:264; *Al-Jarḥ wa't-Taʿdīl*, 4:267; *Majrūḥīn*, 1:344; *Kāmil*, 4:348; *Tārīkh Baghdād*, 9:141; *Mughnī*, 1:273; *Mīzān*, 2:185.

بَاب: جَوَازِ مَنِ انْتَصَرَ مِنْ ظُلْمِهِ إِلَّا الابْنَ وَالْبِنتَ فَشَأْنُهُمَا الإِحْسَان

Chapter: The permissibility to take retribution for injustice, except for the son or daughter, for their concern is benevolence [to their parents]

HADITH 42

عَنْ عَائِشَةَ ﵂ أَنَّ النَّبِيَّ ﷺ قَالَ لَهَا: دُونَكِ فَانْتَصِرِي.

ʿĀ'ishah ﵂ narrates that the Prophet ﷺ said to her, 'Go ahead and take retribution.'[1]

Commentary: The purpose of this chapter is clear. The general rule is that it is lawful to take retribution against someone who has committed injustice, although there is merit and reward in being benevolent and forgiving the perpetrator. Imam Bukhārī suggests that a person's relationship with their parents should be based on benevolence. Therefore, if parents wrong a child, the child should not take retribution, rather forgive.

The hadith cited in this chapter is brief. However, Imam Bukhārī transmits a detailed narration in his *Ṣaḥīḥ* (2581), the summary of which is that the other wives of the Prophet ﷺ demanded justice and equality in regard to the relationship between the Prophet ﷺ and ʿĀ'ishah ﵂. After sending Fāṭimah ﵂ and failing to achieve their goal, they sent Zaynab bint Jaḥsh ﵂ to the Prophet ﷺ, who spoke to him and raised her voice at ʿĀ'ishah ﵂. ʿĀ'ishah ﵂ responded and silenced her.

1 *Al-Adab al-Mufrad* (558), *As-Sunan al-Kubrā li 'n-Nasā'ī* (8914, 8915, 11473), *Sunan Ibn Mājah* (1981).

بَاب: مِنَ الإِحْسَانِ وَالمَوَدَّةِ أَنْ تُصَرِّحَ لِمَنْ تُحِبُّ بِأَنَّكَ تُحِبُّهُ وَلاَ سِيَّمَا الْوَالِدِ

Chapter: It is from benevolence and affection that you explicitly mention to whom you love that you love them, especially the parent

HADITH 43

عَنِ الْمِقْدَامِ بْنِ مَعْدِيْ كَرِبَ ﵁ وَكَانَ قَدْ أَدْرَكَهُ قَالَ: قَالَ النَّبِيُّ ﷺ: إِذَا أَحَبَّ أَحَدُكُمْ أَخَاهُ فَلْيُعْلِمْهُ أَنَّهُ أَحَبَّهُ.

Miqdām ibn Maʿdī Karib ﵁—who met the Prophet ﷺ—narrates, 'The Prophet ﷺ said, "When one of you loves his brother, he should inform him that he loves him."'[1]

Commentary: This is because it will make them happy and also increase the love between them. A narration transmitted in the *Musnad* of Aḥmad (21294, 21514) with a weak chain from Abū Dharr ﵁ states that the Prophet ﷺ said, 'When one of you loves his colleague, then he should visit him in his house and inform him that he loves him for the sake of Allah; and I love you, which is why I have come to you in your house.'

1 *Al-Adab al-Mufrad* (542), *Musnad Aḥmad* (17171), *Sunan Abī Dāwūd* (5124), *Jāmiʿ at-Tirmidhī* (2570), *As-Sunan al-Kubrā li 'n-Nasā'ī* (10034), *Ṣaḥīḥ Ibn Ḥibbān* (570), *Al-Mustadrak ʿalā aṣ-Ṣaḥīḥayn* (4:189).

بَاب

Chapter

HADITH 44

سَمِعْتُ مُوْسَى بْنَ إِسْمَاعِيْلَ [يَقُوْلُ:] سَمِعْتُ أَبَا عَاصِمٍ يَقُوْلُ: مَا اغْتَبْتُ أَحَداً مُنْذُ عَلِمْتُ أَنَّ الْغِيْبَةَ تَضُرُّ أَهْلَهَا.

I heard Mūsā ibn Ismāʿīl say, 'I heard Abū ʿĀṣim say, "I have never backbitten anyone since I learnt that backbiting harms its perpetrators."'[1]

HADITH 45

عَنْ مُعَاوِيَةَ بْنِ قُرَّةَ عَنْ أَبِيْهِ ﵁ قَالَ: قَالَ رَجُلٌ: يَا رَسُوْلَ اللهِ، إِنِّي لَأَذْبَحُ الشَّاةَ وَأَنَا أَرْحَمُهَا، أَوْ: إِنِّي لَأَرْحَمُ الشَّاةَ أَنْ أَذْبَحَهَا، قَالَ: وَالشَّاةُ إِنْ رَحِمْتَهَا يَرْحَمْكَ اللهُ، مَرَّتَيْنِ.

Muʿāwiyah ibn Qurrah narrates from his father ﵁, who said, 'A man said, "O Messenger of Allah, whenever I slaughter a goat, I feel compassionate towards it," or [he said], "I have compassion on the goat [preventing me] from slaughtering it." He ﷺ said twice, "And if you are compassionate to [even] the goat, Allah will be compassionate to you."' *Al-Adab al-Mufrad* (373), *Musnad Aḥmad* (15592, 20363).

---

1 *Khalq Afʿāl al-ʿIbād* (168), *At-Tārīkh al-Kabīr* (4:336), *At-Tawbīkh wa 't-Tanbīh* (167), *At-Targhīb wa 't-Tarhīb* (2244).

HADITH 46

عَنْ نَوَّاسِ بْنِ سِمْعَانَ الأَنْصَارِيِّ ﵁ أَنَّهُ سَأَلَ رَسُوْلَ اللهِ ﷺ عَنِ الْبِرِّ وَالإِثْمِ، فَقَالَ: الْبِرُّ حُسْنُ الْخُلُقِ، وَالإِثْمُ مَا حَكَّ فِي نَفْسِكَ فَكَرِهْتَ أَنْ يَطَّلِعَ عَلَيْهِ النَّاسُ.

Nawwās ibn Samʿān ﵁ narrates that he asked the Messenger of Allah ﷺ about piety and sin. He said, 'Piety is good character, and sin is that which rankles in your heart so that you dislike other people becoming aware of it.'[1]

HADITH 47

عَنِ ابْنِ عُمَرَ ﵄ قَالَ: سَمِعْتُ رَسُوْلَ اللهِ ﷺ وَهُوَ عَلَى الْمِنْبَرِ يَقُوْلُ: أَلَا إِنَّ الْفِتْنَةَ هُنَا يُشِيْرُ إِلَى الْمَشْرِقِ مِنْ حَيْثُ يَطْلُعُ قَرْنُ الشَّيْطَانِ.

Ibn ʿUmar ﵄ narrates, 'I heard Allah's Messenger ﷺ saying whilst he was on the pulpit, "Beware, indeed turmoil (*fitnah*) will appear from here," pointing towards the east, "from where the horn of the devil will appear."'[2]

Commentary: In this chapter, Imam Bukhārī has transmitted some miscellaneous narrations that emphasise the importance of showing mercy, adopting good character and manners and avoiding backbiting.

The final hadith requires explanation. A narration in *Ṣaḥīḥ al-Bukhārī* (1037) suggests that the horn of the devil will appear from Najd. Najd refers to the highland region beyond Hejaz towards Iraq (*Nihāyah*, 5:18.) which is to the east of the blessed city of Madīnah. The term '*qarn*' (horn) is a reference to the head of the devil (*Taʾwīl Mukhtalif al-Ḥadīth*, 1:196) or his army and group. (*Sharḥ Ibn Baṭṭāl ʿalā*

1 *Al-Adab al-Mufrad* (295, 302), *Ṣaḥīḥ Muslim* (2553), *Ṣaḥīḥ Ibn Ḥibbān* (397).

2 *Ṣaḥīḥ al-Bukhārī* (3279), *Ṣaḥīḥ Muslim* (2905).

Ṣaḥīḥ al-Bukhārī, 3:28). The Prophet ﷺ warned that turmoil will appear from this region. This is most probably referring to the turmoil that occurred after the death of ʿUthmān, after which the Muslim's ranks split and deviant sects emerged.[1] Another possibility is that it is a reference to the emergence of the Dajjāl (Anti-Christ), as some narrations suggest that he will emerge from Kufa in Iraq. (*Sharḥ Ibn Baṭṭāl ʿalā Ṣaḥīḥ al-Bukhārī*, 3:28). Either way, the relevance of this hadith to the subject matter of the book is not entirely clear. Perhaps Imam Bukhārī is indicating that this turmoil will open the door for many trials and tribulations until the Day of Judgement, including the *fitnah* of disobedience to parents, which has been referred to as one of the signs of the Final Hour, [2] as mentioned by Imam Bukhārī in the chapter after the next.

1 Ibid., 10:44; *Istidhkār*, 8:519.

2 *Ṣaḥīḥ Muslim* (8)

بَاب: اَلْخُصُوْمَةُ فِي الدُّنْيَا تُكَرَّرُ لِلْحِسَابِ يَوْمَ الْقِيَامَةِ فَاحْذَرْ مِنْهَا وَلاَ سِيَّمَا مَعَ الْوَالِدَيْنِ

Chapter: Disputes in this world will be repeated for reckoning on the Day of Resurrection, so be wary of them, especially with parents

HADITH 48

عَنْ عَبْدِ اللهِ بْنِ الزُبَيْرِ ﵄ قَالَ: قَالَ الزُبَيْرُ ﵁: لَمَّا نَزَلَتْ ﴿ثُمَّ إِنَّكُمْ يَوْمَ الْقِيَامَةِ عِنْدَ رَبِّكُمْ تَخْتَصِمُوْنَ﴾ قَالَ الزُّبَيْرُ: يَا رَسُوْلَ اللهِ، يُكَرَّرُ عَلَيْنَا الْخُصُوْمَةُ بَعْدَ الَّذِيْ كَانَ لَنَا فِي الدُّنْيَا؟ قَالَ: نَعَمْ، قُلْتُ: إِنَّ الأَمْرَ لَشَدِيْد.

ʿAbdullāh ibn az-Zubayr ﵄ narrates, 'Zubayr ﵁ said, "When [the following verse] was revealed: *'Then indeed, on the Day of Resurrection, you will be disputing before your Lord,'.*[1] Zubayr said, "O Messenger of Allah, our disputes will be repeated to us after what has happened between us in this world?" He said, "Yes," so I said, "Indeed, the matter is most serious."'[2]

1 Qur'an (39:31).

2 *Musnad Aḥmad* (60), *Musnad al-Ḥumaydī* (60), *Jāmiʿ at-Tirmidhī* (3236), *Al-Mustadrak ʿalā aṣ-Ṣaḥīḥayn*, 2:272.

HADITH 49

عَنْ عَبْدَ اللهِ بْنِ الزُبَيْرِ ﷺ يَقُوْلُ: لَمَّا نَزَلَتْ ﴿ثُمَّ إِنَّكُمْ يَوْمَ الْقِيَامَةِ عِنْدَ رَبِّكُمْ تَخْتَصِمُوْنَ﴾ قَالَ الزُّبَيْرُ: يَا رَسُوْلَ اللهِ يُكَرَّرُ عَلَيْنَا مَا كَانَ مِنَّا فِي الدُّنْيَا مَعَ خَوَاصِّ الذُّنُوْبِ؟ قَالَ: نَعَمْ، لَيُكَرَّرَنَّ عَلَيْكُمْ حَتَّى يُؤَدَّى إِلَى كُلِّ ذِيْ حَقٍّ حَقُّهُ، قَالَ الزُّبَيْرُ: وَاللهِ إِنَّ الأَمْرَ لَشَدِيْد.

ʿAbdullāh ibn az-Zubayr ﷺ narrates, 'When [the following verse] was revealed: "*Then indeed, on the Day of Resurrection, you will be disputing before your Lord,*" (Qur'an (39:31)). Zubayr said, "O Messenger of Allah, what happened between us in this world will be repeated to us, including even the most intrinsic of sins?" He said, "Yes, they will be repeated to you until every rightful person is given his due." Zubayr said, "By Allah, indeed the matter is most serious."'[1]

HADITH 50

عَنِ ابْنِ عُمَرَ ﷺ قَالَ: لَمَّا نَزَلَتْ ﴿ثُمَّ إِنَّكُمْ يَوْمَ الْقِيَامَةِ عِنْدَ رَبِّكُمْ تَخْتَصِمُوْنَ﴾ لَمْ نَدْرِيْ مَا تَفْسِيْرُهَا، فَلَمَّا وَقَعَتِ الْفِتْنَةُ قُلْنَا: هذَا الَّذِيْ وَعَدَنَا رَبُّنَا أَنْ نَخْتَصِمَ فِيْه.

Ibn ʿUmar ﷺ said, 'When [the following verse] was revealed: "*Then indeed, on the Day of Resurrection, you will be disputing before your Lord,*" (Qur'an (39:31)). we did not know its interpretation. Then when the turmoil (*fitnah*) occurred, we said, "This is what our Lord promised us we would be disputing about."'[2]

---

1 See footnote 30.

2 *Tārīkh al-Madīnah* (2347), *Tafsīr aṭ-Ṭabarī* (21:287), *As-Sunan al-Kubrā li 'n-Nasā'ī* (11447), *Sharḥ Mushkil al-Āthār* (1:123), *Tafsīr Ibn Abī Ḥātim* (10:3250).

Commentary: ʿAbdullāh ibn ʿUmar ﷺ realised the interpretation of this verse following the turmoil and disputes among the Companions because there were previously no such disputes in the Prophet's ﷺ era or thereafter, until the killing of ʿUthmān ﷺ. This does not mean that the verse is specific to the Companions, rather as Imam Ibn Jarīr at-Ṭabarī affirms in *Jāmiʿ al-Bayān* (20:202), the verse is general and applies to all humans. Imam Bukhārī's message through this chapter is clear: a person should not dispute with his parents because disputes will be repeated on the Day of Judgement and result in humiliation.

بَاب: تَكْثُرُ الْفِتَنُ فِيْآخِرِ الزَّمَانِ وَلاَ سِيَّمَا عُقُوْقُ الْوَالِدَيْنِ

Chapter: Turmoils will increase towards the end of time, especially disobedience of parents

HADITH 51

عَنْ أُسَامَةَ بْنِ زَيْدٍ ﵄ أَنَّ النَّبِيَّ ﷺ قَالَ: هَلْ تَرَوْنَ مَا أَرَى، أَرَى الْفِتَنَ تَقَعُ خِلاَلَ بُيُوْتِكُمْ.

Usāmah ibn Zayd ﵄ narrates that the Prophet ﷺ said, 'Do you see what I see? I see turmoils occurring between your homes.' *Ṣaḥīḥ al-Bukhārī* (1878, 3597, 7060).

HADITH 52

عَنْ أُسَامَةَ ﵁ قَالَ: قَالَ النَّبِيُّ ﷺ: هَلْ تَرَوْنَ مَا أَرَى، إِنِّي لأَرَى مَوَاقِعَ الْفِتَنِ خِلاَلَ بُيُوتِكُمْ كَمَوَاقِعِ الْقَطْرِ.

Usāmah [ibn Zayd ﵄] narrates, 'The Prophet ﷺ said, "Do you see what I see? I see turmoils occurring between your houses like droplets of rain."'[1]

Commentary: Reference to the turmoil after the killing of ʿUthmān ﵁ was made earlier and it was mentioned that this opened the door

1 *Ṣaḥīḥ al-Bukhārī* (2467, 7060), *Ṣaḥīḥ Muslim* (2885).

for further trials and tribulations until the Day of Judgement. Imam Nawawī (*Minhāj*, 18:8) and others suggest that these narrations refer to the conflict between the Companions. It appears from the chapter heading that, according to Imam Bukhārī, these narrations refer to the turmoils towards the end of time, although it could be argued otherwise.

Several narrations suggest that disobedience of parents is one of the signs of the Final Hour. For example, a narration in *Ṣaḥīḥ Muslim* (8) suggests that the signs of the Final Hour include that a slave-girl will give birth to her master. One interpretation of this is disobedience of mothers, as mentioned by Qāḍī ʿIyāḍ in *Ikmāl al-Muʿlim*, 1:205 and others.

بَاب

Chapter

HADITH 53

عَنْ كُرْزَ بْنِ عَلْقَمَةَ ﵁ قَالَ: قَالَ أَعْرَابِيٌّ لِلنَّبِيِّ ﷺ: هَلْ لِلإِسْلَامِ مُنْتَهى؟ قَالَ: نَعَمْ، أَيُّمَا أَهْلِ بَيْتٍ مِنَ الْعَرَبِ أَوِ الْعَجَمِ أَرَادَ اللهُ بِهِمْ خَيْرًا أَدْخَلَ عَلَيْهِم الإِسْلَامَ ثُمَّ تَقَعُ الْفِتَنُ كَأَنَّهَا الظُّلَمُ، فَقَالَ الأَعْرَابِيُّ: كَلَّا، قَالَ: بَلَى، وَالَّذِيْ نَفْسِيْ بِيَدِهِ ثُمَّ تَعُوْدُوْنَ فِيْهَا أَسَاوِدَ صُبًّا يَضْرِبُ بَعْضُكُمْ رِقَابَ بَعْضٍ.

Kurz ibn ʿAlqamah ﵁ narrates, 'A bedouin asked the Prophet ﷺ, "Is there a limit for [the spreading of] Islam?" He [ﷺ] said, "Yes. Whichever household Allah intends good for, Arab or non-Arab, He causes Islam to enter. Then turmoils will occur as though they are darknesses." The bedouin then remarked, "Not at all [i.e. this will not occur]." He [ﷺ] said, "Certainly [it will occur]. By the One in whose Hand is my soul, you will then return therein as black snakes, some of you striking the necks of others."'[1]

---

1 *Musnad Aḥmad* (10917, 10918); *Al-Muʿjam al-Kabīr*, 19:197); *Al-Mustadrak ʿalā aṣ-Ṣaḥīḥayn*, 4:502.

HADITH 54

عَنْ عَبْدِ اللهِ [ابْنِ عُمَرَ ﵄] أَنَّهُ سَمِعَ رَسُوْلَ اللهِ ﷺ وَهُوَ مُسْتَقْبِلُ الْمَشْرِقِ يَقُوْلُ: أَلَا إِنَّ الْفِتْنَةَ هَاهُنَا، أَلَا إِنَّ الْفِتْنَةَ هَاهُنَا، مِنْ حَيْثُ يَطْلُعُ قَرْنُ الشَّيْطَانِ.

ʿAbdullāh [ibn ʿUmar] ﵄ narrates that he heard Allah's Messenger ﷺ whilst he was facing the east, saying, 'Beware, turmoil will appear from here; beware, turmoil will appear from here, from where the horn of the devil will appear.'[1]

Commentary: This chapter is related to the previous few chapters pertaining to turmoils and tribulations. Ḥāfiẓ Ibn Rajab explains in *Fatḥ al-Bārī* (1:109) that the term '*asāwid*' is the plural of '*aswad*,' which is the deadliest and biggest snake. Accordingly, when the turmoil occurred, Muslims fought one another and many were killed. The hadith also suggests that turmoils hinder the spreading of Islam.

1 *Ṣaḥīḥ al-Bukhārī* (7092) (7093); see also: footnotes 30 and 31.

بَاب: عُقُوْبَةِ قَاطِعِ الرَّحِمِ فِي الدُّنْيَا

Chapter: The punishment in this world for the person who severs ties of kinship

HADITH 55

عَنْ أَبِيْ بَكْرَةَ ﵁ قَالَ: قَالَ النَّبِيُّ ﷺ: مَا مِنْ ذَنْبٍ أَحْرَى أَنْ يُعَجِّلَ اللهُ لِصَاحِبِهِ الْعُقُوبَةَ فِي الدُّنْيَا مَعَ مَا يُدَّخَرُ لَهُ فِي الْآخِرَةِ مِنْ قَطِيعَةِ الرَّحِمِ وَالْبَغْيِ.

Abū Bakrah ﵁ narrates, 'The Prophet ﷺ said, "There is no sin which Allah is swifter to punish in this world, in addition to the punishment which is accumulated for him in the Hereafter, than the [sin of] severing ties of kinship and injustice."'[1]

HADITH 56

عَنْ أَبِيْ هُرَيْرَةَ ﵁ قَالَ: أَتَى رَجُلٌ النَّبِيَّ ﷺ فَقَالَ: إِنَّ لِيْ قَرَابَةً أَصِلُهُمْ وَيَقْطَعُوْنَ، وَأَحْلُمُ عَنْهُمْ وَيَجْهَلُوْنَ عَلَيَّ وَأُحْسِنُ إِلَيْهِمْ وَيُسِيْئُوْنَ إِلَيَّ، قَالَ: لَئِنْ كَانَ كَمَا تَقُوْلُ كَأَنَّهُمْ تُسِفُّهُمُ الْمَلَّ، فَلاَ يَزَالُ مَعَكَ مِنَ اللهِ ظَهِيْرٌ مَا دُمْتَ عَلَى ذَلِكَ.

Abū Hurayrah ﵁ narrates, 'A man came to the Prophet ﷺ and said,

1 *Al-Adab al-Mufrad* (29, 67), *Sunan Abī Dāwūd* (4904), *Jāmiʿ at-Tirmidhī* (2511), *Sunan Ibn Mājah* (4211), *Ṣaḥīḥ Ibn Ḥibbān* (455).

"Indeed, I have relatives with whom I maintain ties of kinship, whilst they sever them; I am forbearing to them and they behave ignorantly towards me; and I am good to them, whilst they are bad to me." He ﷺ said, "If things are as you say, it is as though you are feeding them hot embers, and there will always be support from Allah with you as long as you continue to do that." *Al-Adab al-Mufrad* (52), *Muslim* (2558).

HADITH 57

عَنْ عَبْدِ اللهِ بْنِ عَمْرٍو رضي الله عنهما عَنِ النَّبِيِّ ﷺ قَالَ: لَيْسَ الْوَاصِلُ بِالْمُكَافِئِ، وَلَكِنَّ الْوَاصِلَ الَّذِيْ إِذَا تَوَلَّتْ رَحِمُهُ وَصَلَهَا.

ʿAbdullāh ibn ʿAmr رضي الله عنهما narrates from the Prophet ﷺ, who said, 'The person who maintains ties of kinship is not someone who [merely] reciprocates. Rather, the person who maintains ties of kinship is someone who maintains ties when his kin turns away [from him].'[1]

Commentary: The punishment in the Hereafter for the person who severs ties of kinship has already been mentioned. This chapter focuses on the consequences in this world. Severing ties of kinship is amongst those sins that result in punishment in this world, similar to oppression. Mullā ʿAlī al-Qārī (d. 1014/1605) suggests in *Mirqāt* (7:3091) that the term '*baghy*' (translated above as 'oppression') could signify oppression, rebellion against the leader or displaying pride. A narration transmitted by Imam Ibn Lāl (d. 398/1007–8) suggests, in *Makārim al-Akhlāq*, that there are five sins which Allah is swifter to punish in this world: oppression, treachery, disobedience of parents, severing ties of kinship and ungratefulness. (*Fayḍ al-Qadīr*, 3:459).

In relation to the hot embers mentioned in the second narration,

1 *Al-Adab al-Mufrad* (68), also see footnote 17.

Qāḍī ʿIyāḍ writes in *Ikmāl al-Muʿlim* (8:22), 'It means that, through your benevolence to them, you are putting them to shame.' It could also be a reference to the spiritual harm caused to those who sever ties of kinship just as hot embers harm the body, (*Ifṣāḥ*, 8:184) or it could be a reference to the punishment of hellfire.

The third narration has been discussed previously. See the Commentary on Hadith 28.

بَاب: فَضْلِ مَنْ يَصِلُ ذَا الرَّحِمِ الظَّالِمَ

Chapter: The virtue of someone who maintains ties with an oppressive relative

HADITH 58

عَنِ الْبَرَاءِ ﵁ قَالَ: جَاءَ أَعْرَابِيٌّ فَقَالَ: يَا نَبِيَّ اللهِ، عَلِّمْنِيْ عَمَلاً يُدْخِلُنِي الْجَنَّةَ، قَالَ: لَئِنْ كُنْتَ أَقْصَرْتَ الْخُطْبَةَ لَقَدْ أَعْرَضْتَ الْمَسْأَلَةَ، أَعْتِقِ النَّسَمَةَ وَفُكَّ الرَّقَبَةَ، قَالَ: أَوَ لَيْسَتَا وَاحِدٌ؟ قَالَ: لاَ، عِتْقُ النَّسَمَةِ أَنْ تُعْتِقَ النَّسَمَةَ وَفَكُّ الرَّقَبَةِ أَنْ تُعِيْنَ عَلَى الرَّقَبَةِ، وَالْمَنِيْحَةُ الْوَكُوْف، وَالْفَيْءُ عَلَى ذِي الرَّحِمِ الظَّالِمِ، فَإِنْ لَمْ تُطِقْ فَتَأْمُرْ بِالْمَعْرُوْفِ وَانْهَ عَنِ الْمُنْكَرِ، فَإِنْ لَمْ تُطِقْ فَكُفَّ لِسَانَكَ إِلاَّ مِنْ خَيْرٍ.

Barā' ﵁ narrates, 'A bedouin came and said, "O Prophet of Allah! Teach me an action that will enter me into Paradise." He [ﷺ] said, "You have asked a broad question, even though your remark was succinct. Free a soul and set a slave free." He said, "Are they not the same?" He [ﷺ] said, "No. Freeing a soul is that you free a soul [yourself] and setting a slave free is to support [or contribute to] his freedom. Also, gifting an animal full of milk, and maintaining good ties with an oppressive relative. If you are unable to do that, then enjoin good and forbid evil. If you are unable to do that, then restrain your tongue from everything except that which is good." *Al-Adab al-Mufrad* (69), *Ṣaḥīḥ Ibn Ḥibbān* (374).

HADITH 59

عَنْ حَكِيْمِ بْنِ حِزَامٍ ﵁ أَنَّهُ قَالَ لِرَسُوْلِ اللهِ ﷺ: أَرَأَيْتَ أُمُوْرًا كُنْتُ أَتَحَنَّثُ بِهَا فِي الْجَاهِلِيَّةِ مِنْ صِلَةٍ وَعَتَاقَةٍ وَصَدَقَةٍ هَلْ لِيْ فِيْهَا أَجْرٌ، قَالَ حَكِيْمٌ: قَالَ رَسُوْلُ اللهِ ﷺ: أَسْلَمْتَ عَلَى مَا سَلَفَ مِنْ خَيْرٍ.

Ḥakīm ibn Ḥizām ﵁ narrates that he said to the Messenger of Allah ﷺ, 'Do you think there is any reward for the deeds I performed in the Time of Ignorance (*Jāhiliyyah*), such as maintaining ties, freeing a slave or charity?' Ḥakīm narrates, 'The Messenger of Allah ﷺ said, "You became a Muslim with all the previous good deeds." *Ṣaḥīḥ al-Bukhārī* (1436, 2220, 2538, 5992), *Ṣaḥīḥ Muslim* (123).

Commentary: The first narration refers to maintaining ties with a relative who has wronged a person. The Prophet ﷺ is reported to have said, 'O ʿUqbah ibn ʿĀmir, maintain [ties of kinship] with he who severs [relations with] you, give to the one who deprives you and forgive the one who oppresses you.' *Musnad Aḥmad* (17452), *Shuʿab al-Īmān* (7723).

The second narration suggests that a revert to Islam benefits and attains the reward of good actions undertaken prior to accepting Islam. This is through the grace of Almighty Allah, because the worship of a non-believer is not valid. Thus, by accepting Islam, Allah forgives all previous sins and provides reward for all previous good actions. *Sharḥ Ibn Baṭṭāl ʿalā Ṣaḥīḥ al-Bukhārī*, 3:437. Some scholars suggest that the narration is merely referring to the fact that it is through the blessings and effects of the actions undertaken in the state of disbelief that Allah guided this person to Islam, and accordingly, those actions are not void of benefit; or that the positive recognition the person acquired as a result of those deeds, and the legacy, shall continue in the state of Islam. (*Ikmāl al-Muʿlim*, 1:415). Either way, this affirms the benefit of maintaining ties of kinship for a non-Muslim.

بَاب: فَضْلِ النَّفَقَةِ وَالصَّدَقَةِ عَلَى الأَقْرَبِيْنَ

Chapter: The virtue of spending on and being charitable to relatives

HADITH 60

عَنْ مَيْمُوْنَةَ ﵂ زَوْجِ النَّبِيِّ ﷺ أَنَّهَا أَعْتَقَتْ جَارِيَةً لَهَا، فَدَخَلَ عَلَيْهَا رَسُوْلُ اللهِ ﷺ فَذَكَرَتْ لَهُ، فَقَالَ: آجَرَكِ اللهُ، أَمَا إِنَّكِ لَوْ أَعْطَيْتِهَا أَخْوَالَكِ كَانَ أَعْظَمَ لِأَجْرِكِ.

Maymūnah ﵂, the wife of the Prophet ﷺ, narrates that she had a slave girl and set her free. When the Messenger of Allah ﷺ came to her, she informed him. He said, 'May Allah reward you for it; if you had gifted her to your maternal uncles, your reward would have been greater.'[1]

Commentary: Imam Bukhārī suggests that spending on relatives is a means of great reward, because a person receives the reward of charity as well as that of maintaining ties of kinship and fulfilling the rights of relatives, particularly if they are in need. The Prophet ﷺ said, as transmitted via authentic chains, 'Giving charity to a poor person is charity and [giving] to a relative is charity and upholding ties of kinship.'[2] In the context of the narration of this chapter, the virtue and reward of this is understood by reflecting on the virtue of

1 *Sunan Abī Dāwūd* (1690), *Musnad Aḥmad* (26817), *Musnad Isḥāq* (2029), *As-Sunan al-Kubrā li 'n-Nasā'ī* (4932), *Al-Muʿjam al-Kabīr* (1066).

2 *Sunan at-Tirmidhī* (658); *Sunan an-Nasā'ī* (2582); *Sunan Ibn Mājah* (1844); *Ṣaḥiḥ Ibn Khuzaymah* (2067); *Ṣaḥīḥ Ibn Ḥibbān*, 8:133.

freeing a slave mentioned earlier in this book (that Allah frees every part of the body from hellfire). This is why ʿAllāmah Ibn Baṭṭāl suggests in *Sharḥ Ṣaḥīḥ al-Bukhārī*, 7:111 that this narration proves that maintaining ties of kinship is more virtuous than freeing slaves. In fact, Qāḍī ʿIyāḍ quotes in *Ikmāl al-Muʿlim*, 8:22 from Imam Mālik, who said, 'Charity on relatives is more virtuous than freeing slaves.' Qāḍī ʿIyāḍ adds that the reason why the Prophet ﷺ specified maternal uncles in this hadith is perhaps because they were in need. This is probably why Ḥāfiẓ Ibn Ḥajar (d. 852/1149) maintains in *Fatḥ al-Bārī* (5:219) that this rule is not absolute. Thus, the superiority of spending on relatives is when they are in need and there could be occasions wherein it is superior to spend on non-relatives. Shaykh al-Islām Ibn Taymiyyah concludes, *Majmūʿ al-Fatāwā*, 29:177. 'Supporting a needy relative is more virtuous than freeing slaves. Imam Aḥmad [d. 241/855] has explicitly mentioned this.'

Note: Zakat cannot be given to parents, children or one's wife, according to the consensus of scholars, as mentioned by Imam Ibn al-Mundhīr (d. 318/930–1). (*Ijmāʿ*, p. 15). However, zakat can be given to other relatives, such as uncles and cousins. There is a difference of opinion in relation to a wife giving zakat to her husband.

بَاب: صِلَةِ الرَّحِمِ وَتَحْرِيْمِ قَطِيْعَتِهَا

Chapter: Enjoining ties of kinship and the prohibition of severing them

HADITH 61

عَنْ أَبِيْ هُرَيْرَةَ ﷺ عَنِ النَّبِيِّ ﷺ قَالَ: إِنَّ اللهَ خَلَقَ الْخَلْقَ حَتَّى إِذَا فَرَغَ مِنْ خَلْقِهِ قَالَتِ الرَّحِمُ: هَذَا مَقَامُ الْعَائِذِ بِكَ مِنَ الْقَطِيْعَةِ، قَالَ: نَعَمْ، أَلاَ تَرْضَيْنَ أَنْ أَصِلَ مَنْ وَصَلَكِ وَأَقْطَعَ مَنْ قَطَعَكِ؟ قَالَتْ: بَلَى يَا رَبِّ، قَالَ: فَهُوَ لَكِ، قَالَ رَسُوْلُ اللهِ ﷺ: إِقْرَؤُوْا إِنْ شِئْتُمْ: ﴿فَهَلْ عَسَيْتُمْ إِنْ تَوَلَّيْتُمْ أَنْ تُفْسِدُوْا فِي الأَرْضِ وَتُقَطِّعُوْا أَرْحَامَكُمْ، أُولَٰئِكَ الَّذِينَ لَعَنَهُمُ اللهُ فَأَصَمَّهُمْ وَأَعْمَىٰ أَبْصَارَهُمْ﴾.

Abū Hurayrah ﷺ narrates from the Prophet ﷺ, who said, 'Indeed, Allah created the creation and at the point when He had completed it, the ties of kinship said, "This is the place for anyone seeking refuge in You from being severed." He [Allah The Most Exalted] said, "Are you not content that I will enjoin the one who enjoins you and I will sever the one who severs you?" It replied, "Yes indeed, my Lord." He said, "Then you have that."' Allah's Messenger ﷺ then said, 'Recite if you wish: "*So would you perhaps, if you turn away, cause corruption on Earth and sever your ties of kinship? Those are the ones whom Allah has cursed, so He made them deaf and blinded their eyes.*" (Qur'an 47:22–23)[1]

1 *Ṣaḥīḥ al-Bukhārī* (5987, 7502) *Al-Adab al-Mufrad* (50) *Ṣaḥīḥ Muslim* (2554).

HADITH 62

قَالَتْ عَائِشَةُ رضي الله عنها: فَرَجَعَ رَسُوْلُ اللهِ ﷺ إِلَى خَدِيْجَةَ تَرْجُفُ بَوَادِرُهُ، فَدَخَلَ وَقَالَ: زَمِّلُوْنِيْ زَمِّلُوْنِيْ، فَلَمَّا سُرِّيَ عَنْهُ قَالَ لِخَدِيْجَةَ: أَشْفَقْتُ عَلَى نَفْسِيْ، قَالَتْ خَدِيْجَةُ: أَبْشِرْ، فَوَاللهِ لاَ يُخْزِيْكَ اللهُ أَبَدًا، إِنَّكَ لَتَصْدُقُ الْحَدِيْثَ وَتَصِلُ الرَّحِمَ وَتَحْمِلُ الْكَلَّ وَتَقْرِي الضَّيْفَ وَتُعِينُ عَلَى نَوَائِبِ الْحَقِّ، فَانْطَلَقَتْ بِهِ خَدِيْجَةُ إِلَى وَرَقَةَ بْنَ نَوْفَلِ بْنِ أَسَدِ وَكَانَ تَنَصَّرَ شَيْخٌ أَعْمَى يَقْرَأُ الإِنْجِيْلَ بِالْعَرَبِيَّةِ، فَقَالَتْ لَهُ خَدِيْجَةُ: أَيْ عَمِّ اسْمَعْ مِنِ ابْنِ أَخِيْكَ، فَقَالَ لَهُ وَرَقَةُ: يَا ابْنَ أَخِيْ مَاذَا تَرَى؟ فَأَخْبَرَهُ خَبَرَ مَا رَأَى، فَقَالَ وَرَقَةُ: هَذَا النَّامُوْسُ الَّذِيْ أَنْزَلَ اللهُ عَلَى مُوسَى يَا لَيْتَنِيْ فِيْهَا جَذَعًا، يَا لَيْتَنِيْ أَكُوْنُ حَيًّا حِيْنَ يُخْرِجُكَ قَوْمُكَ، قَالَ: أَوَمُخْرِجِيَّ هُمْ؟ قَالَ: نَعَمْ، لَمْ يَأْتِ رَجُلٌ بِمَا جِئْتَ بِهِ قَطُّ إِلاَّ عُوْدِيَ، وَإِنْ يُدْرِكْنِي يَوْمُكَ أَنْصُرْكَ نَصْرًا مُؤَزَّرًا.

ʿĀ'ishah رضي الله عنها narrates, 'The Messenger of Allah ﷺ returned to Khadījah رضي الله عنها trembling. He entered and said, "Cover me! Cover me!" Then when his fear dissipated, he ﷺ said to Khadījah, "I feared for my life." Khadījah رضي الله عنها replied, "Glad tidings. I swear by Allah, Allah will never disgrace you. Indeed, you speak the truth, you maintain the ties of kinship and bear the burden [of others], you honour guests and assist those with a deserving need." Then Khadījah took him to Waraqah ibn Nawfal ibn Asad, who had become a Christian, a blind old man who would read the Gospel in Arabic. Khadījah said to him, "O my uncle, listen to your nephew!" Waraqah asked him, "O my nephew! What do you see?" [Allah's Messenger ﷺ] described what he saw. Then Waraqah said, "This is the archangel whom Allah sent to Moses. I wish I were young. I wish I would be alive when your people drive you out." He ﷺ asked, "Will they drive me out?" He replied, "Yes. No one has come with what you have come with without being treated with hostility, and if I remain alive until your day [when this will occur], I will support you strongly."' *Ṣaḥīḥ al-Bukhārī* (3, 4953, 6982), *Ṣaḥīḥ Muslim* (160).

HADITH 63

عَنْ بِلَالِ بْنِ سَعْدٍ رضي الله عنهما عَنْ أَبِيْهِ أَنَّهُ قَالَ: يَا رَسُوْلَ اللهِ مَا لِلْخَلِيْفَةِ مِنْ بَعْدِكَ؟ قَالَ: مِثْلُ الَّذِيْ لِيْ، مَا عَدَلَ فِي الْحُكْمِ وَقَسَطَ فِي الْبَسْطِ وَرَحِمَ ذَا الرَّحِمِ، فَمَنْ فَعَلَ غَيْرَ ذَلِكَ فَلَيْسَ مِنِّيْ وَلَسْتُ مِنْهُ، قَالَ: يُرِيْدُ الطَّاعَةَ فِي طَاعَةِ اللهِ وَالْمَعْصِيَةَ فِيْ مَعْصِيَةِ اللهِ .

Bilāl ibn Saʿd رضي الله عنهما narrates from his father that he said, 'O Messenger of Allah, what is [our duty] to the caliph after you?' He said, 'The same as [your duty] to me, so long as he is just in judgements, fair in distribution and merciful to kin. Whoever does anything besides that, then he is not from me, nor am I from him.' (*At-Tārīkh al-Kabīr* (1915), *Al-Muʿjam al-Kabīr* (5461)). [Saʿd] said, 'He meant obedience [to the caliph] in matters of obedience to Allah and disobedience [of the caliph] in matters of disobedience to Allah.'

Commentary: A shorter version of the first narration has been transmitted by Imam Bukhārī earlier in this collection. The purpose of repeating this narration here is to affirm through the Qur'anic verse that severing ties of kinship is clearly unlawful (*ḥarām*).

The second narration is part of a lengthier one that has been transmitted by Imam Bukhārī in his *Ṣaḥīḥ* (3) describing the first revelation and what happened in the immediate aftermath. The relevant part of the narration is the statement of Khadījah ﷺ wherein she alleviates the Prophet's ﷺ fear by reassuring him that Allah will never disgrace him on account of him maintaining ties of kinship, among other deeds. Therefore, a person who maintains ties of kinship is never disgraced in this world. Khadījah ﷺ believed in this even though at this point she was not aware of Islam's position in relation to maintaining family ties.

The third narration affirms the prohibition of severing ties of kinship. This is because obeying the leader is an obligation, unless they violate divine laws. The Prophet ﷺ said, 'Listening and obeying [the ruler] is necessary, so long as one is not ordered to sin. If he is ordered to sin, then there is no listening or obeying [the leader].' (*Ṣaḥīḥ al-Bukhārī* (2955)). Therefore, a ruler who does not maintain ties of kinship is violating divine laws and distancing himself from the Prophet ﷺ.

بَاب: الأَقْرَبُ فَالأَقْرَبُ

Chapter: The nearest then the nearest [relatives]

HADITH 64

عَنْ جَابِرٍ ﵁ أَنَّهُ قَالَ: أَعْتَقَ رَجُلٌ مِنْ بَنِيْ عُذْرَةَ عَبْدًا لَهُ عَنْ دُبُرٍ، فَبَلَغَ ذَلِكَ رَسُوْلَ اللهِ ﷺ فَقَالَ: لَكَ مَالٌ غَيْرُهُ؟ قَالَ: لاَ، فَقَالَ رَسُوْلُ اللهِ ﷺ: مَنْ يَشْتَرِيهِ مِنِّي؟ فَاشْتَرَاهُ نُعَيْمُ بْنُ عَبْدِ اللهِ النَّحَّام بِثَمَانِمِائَةِ دِرْهَمٍ، فَجَاءَ بِهَا رَسُوْلَ اللهِ ﷺ فَدَفَعَهَا إِلَيْهِ، ثُمَّ قَالَ: ابْدَأْ بِنَفْسِكَ فَتَصَدَّقْ عَلَيْهَا، فَإِنْ فَضَلَ شَيْءٌ فَلأَهْلِكَ، فَإِنْ فَضَلَ عَنْ أَهْلِكَ شَيْءٌ فَلِذِيْ قَرَابَتِكَ، فَإِنْ فَضَلَ عَنْ ذِي قَرَابَتِكَ شَيْءٌ فَهَكَذَا وَهَكَذَا، يَقُوْلُ: بَيْنَ يَدَيْكَ وَعَنْ يَمِيْنِكَ وَعَنْ شِمَالِكَ.

Jābir ﵁ narrates, 'A person from the Banū ʿUdhrah set a *mudabbar* slave free [A *mudabbar* slave is one whose freedom is conditioned upon the master's death]. This news reached the Messenger of Allah ﷺ and he said, "Have you any wealth besides him?" He said, "No." The Messenger of Allah ﷺ said, "Who will purchase him from me?" So Nuʿaym ibn ʿAbdillāh an-Naḥḥām bought him for eight hundred dirhams, which he gave to the Messenger of Allah ﷺ. He [ﷺ] gave it to [the man who had freed the slave] and then said, "Start with yourself and spend it on yourself. If anything is left, then spend on your immediate family. If anything is left after spending on your immediate family, it is for your relatives [i.e. distant family]. If anything is left after spending on your relatives, then spend it in such and such manner," saying, "in front of you, on your right and on your left." *Ṣaḥīḥ al-Bukhārī* (2141, 2403), *Ṣaḥīḥ Muslim* (997).

Commentary: Relatives should be afforded benevolence according to the closeness of the relation. The same principle applies to neighbours; whoever lives closer has a greater right than the one who lives at a distance. Imam Nawawī explains in his commentary on *Ṣaḥīḥ Muslim* (16:103) that after parents, priority is afforded to children, then grandparents, then siblings, then the remaining *maḥārim* (unmarriageable kin), such as uncles, aunts and their spouses; then to one's in-laws, then freed men and then the neighbour, with the closest being prioritised over the furthest.

بَاب: مِنْ أَشْرَاطِ السَّاعَةِ أَن يَفْشُوَ قَطْعُ الأَرْحَامِ

Chapter: From amongst the signs of the Final Hour is that severing of ties of kinship will be widespread

HADITH 65

حَدَّثَنَا سَعِيْدُ بْنُ سَمْعَانَ قَالَ: سَمِعْتُ أَبَا هُرَيْرَةَ ﷺ يَتَعَوَّذُ مِنْ إِمَارَةِ الصِّبْيَانِ وَالسُّفَهَاءِ، فَقَالَ سَعِيْدُ بْنُ سَمْعَانَ: فَأَخْبَرَنِيْ ابْنُ حَسَنَةَ الْجُهَنِيُّ أَنَّهُ قَالَ لأَبِيْ هُرَيْرَةَ: مَا آيَةُ ذَلِكَ؟ قَالَ: أَنْ تُقْطَعَ الأَرْحَامُ وَيُطَاعَ الْمُغْوِي وَيُعْصَى الْمُرْشِدُ.

Saʿīd ibn Samʿān reports, 'I heard Abū Hurayrah ﷺ seeking refuge from the leadership of juveniles and fools.' Saʿīd ibn Samʿān continues, 'Ibn Ḥasanah al-Juhanī informed me that he asked Abū Hurayrah, "What is the sign of this?" He replied, "That the ties of kinship are severed, the misguided leader is obeyed and the guided leader is disobeyed."' *Al-Adab al-Mufrad* (66).

Commentary: Disobedience of parents is a sign of the Final Hour, as previously discussed.

The leadership of juveniles and fools is a veiled reference to the leadership of Yazīd (d. 64/683) (*Fatḥ al-Bārī*, 13:10). Imam Bukhārī transmits a narration in his *Ṣaḥīḥ* (7058) wherein the Prophet ﷺ said, 'Destruction of my followers will be through the hands of young men from Quraysh.' According to most scholars, this is a reference to Banū Umayyah and their leadership (*Ifṣāḥ*, 6:444; *ʿUmdat al-Qārī*, 24:180) and is therefore connected to the narration of this chapter, although Mullā ʿAlī al-Qārī is inclined to the view (*Mirqāt*, 8:3386) that the narration in *Ṣaḥīḥ al-Bukhārī* refers to those who killed ʿUthmān ﷺ.

بَاب: تُبَلُّ الرَّحِمُ بِبِلاَلِهَا

Chapter: Ties of kinship are kept moist with their wetness [i.e. maintained adequately]

HADITH 66

عَنْ عَمْرِو بْنِ الْعَاصِ ﷺ قَالَ: سَمِعْتُ رَسُوْلَ اللهِ ﷺ يُنَادِيْ سِرًّا غَيْرَ جَهْرٍ: إِنَّمَا وَلِيِّيَ اللهُ وَالَّذِيْنَ آمَنُوْا وَلَكِنْ لَهُمْ رَحِمٌ سَأَبُلُّهَا بِبِلَالِهَا.

ʿAmr ibn ʿĀṣ ﷺ narrates, 'I heard the Messenger of Allah ﷺ calling out quietly, not loudly, "My friend is only Allah and those who believe; however, they [i.e. non-believers] have a tie of kinship [with me] which I will keep moist with its wetness [i.e. maintain adequately]."' *Ṣaḥīḥ al-Bukhārī* (5644), *Ṣaḥīḥ Muslim* (204).

Commentary: The purpose of this chapter is to highlight that ties of kinship must be maintained with all relatives, even if they are not Muslims. Imam Muhallab explains that friendship should be based on faith and not on kinship. However, this does not mean that a person should neglect maintaining family ties and being dutiful to relatives. (*Sharḥ Ibn Baṭṭāl ʿalā Ṣaḥīḥ al-Bukhārī*, 9:208). Reference has already been made to the story of Asmāʾ ﷺ transmitted in *Ṣaḥīḥ al-Bukhārī* (5979) wherein she asked the Prophet ﷺ regarding her polytheist mother, 'Indeed, my mother has arrived and she is hoping [for my favour].' He ﷺ said, 'Yes, maintain ties with your mother.'

بَاب: الحَذْرِ مِنْ أَن يُقَدِّمَ زَوْجَهُ عَلَى أَبَوَيْهِ

Chapter: The warning for someone who gives preference to his wife over his parents

HADITH 67

عَنْ أُسَامَةَ بْنِ زَيْدٍ ﷺ عَنِ النَّبِيِّ ﷺ قَالَ: مَا تَرَكْتُ بَعْدِي فِتْنَةً أَضَرَّ عَلَى الرِّجَالِ مِنَ النِّسَاءِ.

Usāmah ibn Zayd ﷺ narrates from the Prophet ﷺ, who said, 'I have not left after me a temptation more calamitous to men than women.' *Ṣaḥīḥ al-Bukhārī* (5096), *Ṣaḥīḥ Muslim* (2741).

Commentary: This chapter and the narration transmitted to conclude the book is of particular significance and demonstrates the deep insight and intelligence of Imam Bukhārī. The temptation (*fitnah*) of women referenced in this narration is generally understood to mean fornication and adultery. However, Imam Bukhārī highlights, through the general wording of this narration, that it also includes a husband giving preference to his wife over his parents, which is extremely harmful to his faith. This has sadly become increasingly common nowadays, with some parents being forced out of the house due to pressure from the wife, or in some cases being ridiculed on account of the wife. A hadith transmitted in *Sunan at-Tirmidhī* (2210) via a weak chain states, 'When my Ummah does fifteen things, then afflictions will occur in it.' It was said, 'What are they O Messenger of Allah?' He said, 'When the spoils of war are distributed [preferentially], trust is a spoil of war [and is usurped], zakat is [treated as] a fine, a man obeys his wife and disobeys his mother, he is kind to his friend and abandons his father, voices are raised in the mosques, the leader of the people is the most despicable among them, the man is honoured out of fear of his evil, alcohol is consumed, silk is worn [by males], singing slave-girls and music is common, and the latter of this nation (*Ummah*) curses its former. [When these things occur,] then anticipate a [destructive] red wind or collapsing of the earth and transformation.'

The term '*fitnah*' mentioned in the hadith is, therefore, all encompassing. Shaykh al-Islam Ibn Taymiyyah warns against obeying one's wife in matters of innovation and imitation of disbelievers and mentions that obeying women leads to the fall of empires and corruptness of kingdoms. In *Iqtiḍa'*, 2:6; *Majmūʿ al-Fatāwā*, 25:324 he cites the hadith of the Prophet ﷺ wherein he said to the women, 'I have not seen anyone more deficient in intelligence and religion than one of you, who can overpower [and lead astray] an intelligent man.' (*Ṣaḥīḥ al-Bukhārī* (304)).

May Allah Almighty enable us to appreciate our parents and make us the coolness of their eyes.

APPENDIX 1

Narrations in Ṣaḥīḥ al-Bukhārī not Transmitted in This Book

Imam Bukhārī has transmitted hadiths regarding being dutiful to parents in his *Ṣaḥīḥ*, as well as in *Al-Adab al-Mufrad*. Most of these narrations have also been transmitted in this collection. However, the ones that have not been transmitted have been translated here for the benefit of readers.

CHAPTER: A MAN SHOULD NOT SWEAR AT HIS PARENTS

ʿAbdullāh ibn ʿAmr ﷺ narrates that the Messenger of Allah ﷺ said, 'Indeed, from amongst the greatest of major sins is that a man curses his parents.' It was said, 'O Messenger of Allah, and how does a man curse his parents?' He said, 'The person swears at the father of another person, so he then swears at his father, and he swears at his mother, so he swears at his mother.' *Ṣaḥīḥ al-Bukhārī* (5973).

CHAPTER: THE ACCEPTANCE OF THE SUPPLICATION OF SOMEONE WHO WAS KIND TO HIS PARENTS

Ibn ʿUmar ﷺ narrates from the Messenger of Allah ﷺ that he said, 'Whilst three people were walking, rain began to fall and they took shelter in a mountain cave. A boulder from the mountain rolled over the mouth of the cave and blocked them in. They said to each other, "Look at any pious actions you have performed only for Allah, then invoke Allah with them that He may remove it." So one of them said, "O Allah! I had parents who were very old and I had small children for whose sake I used to work as a shepherd. When I would return to them at night and milk [the livestock], I would begin by giving the milk to my parents first, before giving to my children. One day the grazing delayed me, and I did not return home until the evening and found that my parents had fallen asleep. I milked [my livestock] as usual and brought the milk vessel and stood at their heads. I disliked waking them up from their sleep and I also disliked giving the milk to my children before my parents, though my children were crying at my feet, so this state of mine and theirs continued till dawn broke. [O Allah!] If you consider that I did that only seeking Your pleasure, then please let there be an opening through which we can see the sky." So Allah made for them an opening through which they could see the sky. Then the second person said, "O Allah! I had a cousin whom I loved as much as a man loves a woman. I tried to seduce her, but she refused, until I paid her one hundred dinars. I worked hard until I collected one hundred dinars and went to her with that, but when I sat between her legs, she said, 'O servant of Allah! Fear Allah! Do not deflower the seal except legally.' So I stood up and left her. [O Allah!] If you consider that I did that only seeking Your pleasure, then please create an opening." So Allah widened the opening. Then the last person said, "O Allah! I employed a labourer for wages equal to a certain measure of rice, and when he had finished his job, he said, 'Give me my due,' but when I presented his due to him, he gave it up and refused to take it. Then I kept on sowing that rice for him, until I amassed some cows and their shepherd. [Later on], the labourer came to me and said, 'Fear Allah, do not be unjust to me and give me my due.' So I said, 'Go and take those cows and their shepherd.' He said, 'Fear Allah and do not mock me.' I replied, 'I am not mocking you, take those cows and their shepherd.' So he took them and went away. [O Allah!] If You considered that I did that seeking Your pleasure, then please relieve us from what is left." And so Allah relieved them.' *Ṣaḥīḥ al-Bukhārī* (2215, 5974).

CHAPTER: DISOBEDIENCE OF PARENTS IS FROM THE MAJOR SINS

Mughīrah ﷺ narrates that the Prophet ﷺ said, 'Allah has forbidden to you the disobedience of mothers, withholding [what you owe to others] whilst making demands, and burying daughters alive; and Allah has disliked for you gossip, incessant questioning and squandering wealth.' *Ṣaḥīḥ al-Bukhārī* (5975).

CHAPTER: A MARRIED WOMAN MAINTAINING TIES WITH HER MOTHER

Asmā' ﷺ narrates, 'My mother, who was a polytheist, came with her son during the period of the peace treaty with the Quraysh and their agreement with the Prophet ﷺ, so I went to ask the Prophet ﷺ, saying, 'Indeed, my mother has arrived and she is hoping [for my favour].' He ﷺ said, 'Yes, maintain ties with your mother.' *Ṣaḥīḥ al-Bukhārī* (5979).

APPENDIX 2

Narrations in Al-Adab al-Mufrad not Transmitted in This Book

CHAPTER: THE SPEECH OF ALLAH THE EXALTED:

﴿وَوَصَّيْنَا الْإِنسَانَ بِوَالِدَيْهِ﴾

And We instructed man to be good to his parents. Qur'an (31:14)

ʿAbdullāh ibn ʿUmar ﷺ said, 'The pleasure of the Lord lies in the pleasure of the parent, and the displeasure of the Lord lies in the displeasure of the parent.' *Al-Adab al-Mufrad* (2).

CHAPTER: BEING DUTIFUL TO ONE'S MOTHER

ʿAṭāʾ ibn Yasār narrates that a man came to Ibn ʿAbbās ﷺ and said, 'I proposed to a woman and she refused to marry me. Another man asked her and she agreed to marry him, so I became jealous and killed her. Is there any repentance for me?' He asked, 'Is your mother alive?' 'No' he replied. He said, 'Repent to Allah ﷻ and try to draw near to Him as much as you can.' [The narrator says,] 'So I went and asked Ibn ʿAbbās ﷺ: "Why did you enquire about his mother being alive?" He replied, "I do not know of a deed closer to Allah ﷻ than being dutiful to one's mother." *Al-Adab al-Mufrad* (4).

CHAPTER: BEING DUTIFUL TO ONE'S FATHER

Abū Hurayrah ﷺ narrates that a man came to the Prophet of Allah ﷺ and asked, 'What do you command me?' He replied, 'Be dutiful to your mother.' Then he asked him the same question again and he replied, 'Be dutiful to your mother.' He repeated it again and he replied, 'Be dutiful to your mother.' Then he repeated the question for the fourth time and he replied, 'Be dutiful to your mother.' Then he repeated the question for the fifth time and he said, 'Be dutiful to your father.' *Al-Adab al-Mufrad* (6).

CHAPTER: BEING DUTIFUL TO PARENTS EVEN IF THEY ARE UNJUST

Ibn ʿAbbās ﷺ said, 'There is not a Muslim who has Muslim parents towards whom he is dutiful with the intention of reward, except that Allah will open two gates of Paradise for him. If there is only one [parent], then one [gate will be opened]. If one of them is angry, then Allah will not be pleased with him, until that parent is pleased with him.' He was asked, 'Even if they wrong him?' He said, 'Even if they wrong him.' *Al-Adab al-Mufrad* (7).

CHAPTER: SPEAKING GENTLY TO PARENTS

Ibn Mayyās said, 'I was with the Najdites [a group of Kharijites] when I committed sins which I regarded to be from the major sins. I mentioned that to Ibn ʿUmar ﷺ. He enquired, "What are they?" I replied, "Such and such." He stated, "These are not major sins. There are nine major sins. They are: associating partners with Allah, killing someone, fleeing from the battlefield, slandering a chaste woman, usury, usurping an orphan's property, heresy in the mosque, scoffing, and causing one's parents to weep through disobedience." Ibn ʿUmar ﷺ then said to me, "Do you wish to separate yourself from the Fire and would you like to enter Paradise?" "By Allah, yes!" I replied. He asked, "Are your parents still alive?" I replied, "My mother is." He said, "By Allah, if you speak gently to her and feed her, then you will certainly enter Paradise, as long as you abstain from the major sins."' *Al-Adab al-Mufrad* (8).

CHAPTER: REPAYING PARENTS

Saʿīd ibn Abī Burdah said, 'I heard my father narrate that Ibn ʿUmar ﷺ witnessed a Yemeni man circumambulating [in *ṭawāf*] around the *Kaʿbah,* carrying his mother on his back, saying "Indeed, I am for her, her humble camel, if her mount is frightened, I am not frightened." Then he [the Yemeni man] said, "O Ibn ʿUmar, do you think I have repaid her?" He said, "No, not even a single sigh." Then Ibn ʿUmar performed *ṭawāf*, he came to the station [of Ibrāhīm] and prayed two *rakʿahs*, then he said, "O Ibn Abī Mūsā, verily every two *rakʿahs* expiate whatever is before them."' *Al-Adab al-Mufrad* (11).

Abū Murrah, the freed slave of ʿAqīl, narrates that Marwān would appoint Abū Hurayrah ﷺ as his agent [in Hajj]. When he was in Dhū'l-Ḥulayfah, his mother would be in one house and he another. When he wanted to leave, he would stop at her door and say, 'Peace be upon you, O my mother, and the mercy of Allah and His blessings.' She would say, 'And peace be upon you, O my son, and the mercy of Allah and His blessings.' Then he would say, 'May Allah have mercy on you as you raised me as a child,' so she would say, 'May Allah have mercy on you as you were dutiful to me when I was old.' Whenever he wanted to enter, he would do the same. *Al-Adab al-Mufrad* (12).

CHAPTER: ALLAH CURSES THE PERSON WHO CURSES HIS PARENTS

Abū at-Ṭufayl narrates, "ʿAlī ﷺ was asked, "Did the Prophet ﷺ specify you [i.e. his household] with any [advice] that he had not specified all the other people with?" He said, "The Messenger of Allah ﷺ did not specify anything for us other than what he specified for the people, except that which is in the sheath of my sword. Then he took out a parchment, and written upon it was, "Allah curses the person who slaughters for other than Allah. Allah curses the person who steals a landmark. Allah curses the person who curses his parents. Allah curses the person who gives refuge to an innovator."' *Al-Adab al-Mufrad* (17).

CHAPTER: BEING DUTIFUL TO PARENTS, AS LONG AS IT IS NOT DISOBEDIENCE [TO ALLAH]

Abū 'd-Dardā' ﷺ narrates, 'The Messenger of Allah ﷺ commanded me with nine [actions]: Do not associate anything with Allah, even if you are cut or burned. Do not abandon a prescribed prayer deliberately; anyone who abandons it deliberately will forfeit Allah's protection. Do not drink wine; it is the key to every evil. Obey your parents; if they command you to abandon your worldly possessions, then abandon it for them. Do not contend with those in power, even if you think that you are in the right. Do not flee from the battlefield, even if you are killed while your companions flee. Spend on your family within your means. Do not raise your stick on your family. Inculcate fear of Allah ﷻ in them.' *Al-Adab al-Mufrad* (18).

CHAPTER: WHOEVER IS DUTIFUL TO HIS PARENTS, ALLAH WILL LENGTHEN HIS LIFE

Muʿādh ﷺ narrates that the Prophet ﷺ said, 'Glad tidings to the person who is dutiful to his parents. Allah ﷻ will lengthen his life.' *Al-Adab al-Mufrad* (22).

CHAPTER: ONE MAY NOT SEEK FORGIVENESS FOR HIS POLYTHEIST FATHER

Ibn ʿAbbās said regarding the speech of Allah, '*If any one of them, or both of them, reach old age, do not say to them, "Uff!"* [a word or expression of even slight disapproval],' Qur'an (17:24) that the [following] verse Qur'an (9:113) in *[Sūrat] Barā'ah* abrogated it: '*It is not [befitting] for the Prophet and the believers to seek forgiveness for the polytheists, even if they are kin, after it became clear to them that they are the people of hell.*' *Al-Adab al-Mufrad* (23).

CHAPTER: BEING DUTIFUL TO A POLYTHEIST PARENT

Ibn ʿUmar narrates that ʿUmar saw a silk mantle for sale. He said, 'O Messenger of Allah, purchase this robe and wear it on Fridays and when delegations visit you.' He said, 'Only a person who has no portion [in the next world] would wear this.' Then the Messenger of Allah was given [similar] mantles. He sent one of the mantles to ʿUmar. ʿUmar said, 'How can I wear it when you said what you said about it?' He said, 'I did not give it to you so that you could wear it; rather, you can sell it or give it to someone.' So ʿUmar sent it to a brother of his in Makkah before he became a Muslim. *Al-Adab al-Mufrad* (26); *Ṣaḥīḥ al-Bukhārī* (886).

CHAPTER: PUNISHMENT FOR DISOBEYING PARENTS

ʿImrān ibn Ḥuṣayn narrates that the Messenger of Allah said, 'What do you say about fornication, drinking wine and theft?' We said, 'Allah and His Messenger know best.' He said, 'They are acts of indecency and there is punishment for them. Shall I not inform you of the greatest of the major sins? Associating partners with Allah and disobeying parents.' He had been reclining, then he sat up and said, 'and lying.' *Al-Adab al-Mufrad* (30).

CHAPTER: CRYING OF PARENTS

Ibn ʿUmar ﷺ said, 'Making parents cry is part of disobedience and from the major sins.' *Al-Adab al-Mufrad* (31).

CHAPTER: SUPPLICATION OF PARENTS

Abū Hurayrah ﷺ narrates, 'I heard the Messenger of Allah ﷺ saying, "No newborn has ever spoken in the cradle except ʿIsā son of Maryam ﷺ and the companion of Jurayj." It was said, "O Prophet of Allah, who is the companion of Jurayj?" He replied, "Indeed, Jurayj was a monk in his monastery and there was a shepherd of cows who would come to the lower part of his monastery and there was a woman from the village who would frequent the shepherds. His mother came one day and said, 'O Jurayj,' whilst he was praying. He said to himself, 'My mother or my prayer?' He decided to prefer his prayer over his mother. Then she called him for a second time and he said to himself, 'My mother or my prayer?' He decided to prefer his prayer over his mother. Then she called him for a third time and he said to himself, 'My mother or my prayer?' He decided to prefer his prayer over his mother. When he did not answer her, she said, 'Allah will not allow you to pass away, O Jurayj, until you see the face of immoral women,' then she turned away. Then the aforementioned woman, who had given birth, was brought to the king. He asked, 'From whom [did you bear this child]?' She replied, 'From Jurayj.' He remarked, 'The resident of the monastery?' She replied, 'Yes.' He said, 'Destroy his monastery and bring him to me.' So they struck his monastery with axes until it fell. Then they tied his hand to his neck with rope; then he was taken and made to pass by the immoral women. He saw them and smiled whilst they were looking at him amongst the people. The ruler then said, 'What is this one claiming?' He [Jurayj] replied, 'What does she claim?' He said, 'She claims her child is from you.' He [Jurayj] asked, 'Do you claim this?' She replied, 'Yes.' He asked, 'Where is this child?' They said, 'It is the one in her lap.'

Subsequently, he [Jurayj] faced him and asked, 'Who is your father?' He [miraculously] replied, 'The shepherd of the cattle.' The ruler said, 'Should we make you a monastery out of gold?' He replied, 'No.' He said, 'Out of silver?' He replied, 'No.' He asked, 'Then what should we make it out of?' He replied, 'Return it the way it was.' He [the ruler] enquired, 'What made you smile?' He replied, 'A matter which I recognised. The supplication of my mother [against me] affected me.' Then he informed them [of the whole story]."' *Al-Adab al-Mufrad* (33); *Ṣaḥīḥ al-Bukhārī* (1206, 2483, 3436).

CHAPTER: PRESENTING ISLAM TO A CHRISTIAN MOTHER

Abū Hurayrah ‎ narrates, 'No Jew or Christian heard about me except that they loved me. I wanted my mother to become a Muslim, but she would refuse. I then told her this and she [still] refused. I went to the Prophet ‎ and said, "Supplicate to Allah for her." He supplicated and I went to her. She was inside the door of the house and she said, "O Abū Hurayrah, I have become a Muslim." I informed the Prophet ‎ and I requested, "Supplicate to Allah for me and for my mother." He ‎ said, "O Allah, your servant Abū Hurayrah and his mother, make them beloved to the people."' *Al-Adab al-Mufrad* (34).

CHAPTER: BEING DUTIFUL TO PARENTS AFTER THEIR DEATH

Abū Usayd ‎ narrates, 'We were with the Messenger of Allah ‎ when a man asked, "O Messenger of Allah, is there any act of dutifulness I can perform for my parents after their death?" He [‎] replied, "Yes. There are four things: supplication for them and seeking forgiveness for them, fulfilling their vows, honouring their friends and maintaining those ties of kinship for which you have no relation except through them."' *Al-Adab al-Mufrad* (35).

Abū Hurayrah ‎ said, 'A dead person's status can be elevated after their death. He says, "My Lord, how is this [possible]?" He is told, "Your child sought forgiveness for you."' *Al-Adab al-Mufrad* (36).

Ibn Sīrīn narrates, 'We were with Abū Hurayrah ﷺ one night and he said, "O Allah, forgive Abū Hurayrah and his mother and whoever asks for forgiveness for both of them."' Muḥammad [Ibn Sīrīn] continues, 'We would ask for forgiveness for them so that we would be included in the supplication of Abū Hurayrah.' *Al-Adab al-Mufrad* (37).

Abū Hurayrah ﷺ narrates that the Messenger of Allah ﷺ said, 'When a servant dies, his deeds cease except for three: continuous charity, knowledge that benefits, or a righteous child who supplicates for him.' *Al-Adab al-Mufrad* (38).

Ibn ʿAbbās ﷺ narrates that a man said, 'O Messenger of Allah, my mother died without making a bequest. Will it benefit her if I give alms on her behalf?' He replied, 'Yes.' *Al-Adab al-Mufrad* (39); *Ṣaḥīḥ al-Bukhārī* (2756).

CHAPTER: KINDNESS TO A PERSON WITH WHOM ONE'S FATHER MAINTAINED TIES

Ibn ʿUmar ﷺ narrates that a Bedouin passed by whilst travelling and the father of the Bedouin was a friend of ʿUmar ﷺ. The Bedouin said, 'Are you not the son of such a person?' He said, 'I certainly am.' Then Ibn ʿUmar ordered that he be given a donkey that would follow him, and he removed his turban from his head and gave it to him. Some of those who were with him said, 'Would two dirhams not have sufficed him?' He said, 'The Prophet ﷺ said, "Protect the friendship of your father; do not sever it lest Allah extinguish your light."' *Al-Adab al-Mufrad* (40).

CHAPTER: DO NOT SEVER [TIES] WITH SOMEONE WITH WHOM YOUR FATHER MAINTAINED TIES, LEST YOUR LIGHT BE EXTINGUISHED

ʿUbādah az-Zuraqī narrates, 'I was sat in the mosque of Madīnah with ʿAmr ibn ʿUthmān, then ʿAbdullāh ibn Salām ﷺ passed by us, leaning upon his nephew. Then he [ʿAmr] left the gathering and showed concern for him. Then he [ʿAbdullāh ibn Salām] returned to them and said "What do you wish, ʿAmr ibn ʿUthmān?" twice or thrice. "For, by the One who sent Muḥammad ﷺ with the truth, indeed it is in the book of Allah ﷻ," [he remarked] twice, "Do not sever [ties] with someone with whom your father maintained ties, lest your light be extinguished due to that."' *Al-Adab al-Mufrad* (42).

CHAPTER: LOVE IS INHERITED

One of the Companions of the Prophet ﷺ said, 'I will suffice [in informing] you that the Messenger of Allah ﷺ said, "Love is inherited."' *Al-Adab al-Mufrad* (43).

CHAPTER: A PERSON SHOULD NOT ADDRESS HIS FATHER BY HIS NAME, NOR SIT AHEAD OF HIM, NOR WALK IN FRONT OF HIM

Abū Hurayrah ﷺ saw two men and said to one of them, 'Who is this man to you?' He replied, 'He is my father.' So he said, 'Do not address him by his name, nor walk in front of him, nor sit ahead of him.' *Al-Adab al-Mufrad* (44).

CHAPTER: CAN A MAN ADDRESS HIS FATHER BY HIS TEKNONYM?

Shahr ibn Ḥawshab ﷺ said, 'We went out with Ibn ʿUmar ﷺ, then Sālim [the son of Ibn ʿUmar ﷺ] said, "Greetings, Abā ʿAbd ar-Raḥmān."' *Al-Adab al-Mufrad* (45).

APPENDIX 3

Chains of Transmission and Biography of Narrators

HADITH 1

- Hishām ibn ʿAbd al-Malik al-Bāhilī aṭ-Ṭiyālisī
- Shuʿbah ibn al-Hajjāj al-Azdī
- Walīd ibn al-ʿAyzār al-Kūfī
- Abū ʿAmr ash-Shaybānī Saʿd ibn Iyās al-Kūfī
- ʿAbdullah ibn Masʿūd ibn Ghāfil al-Makkī ﵁:

ʿAbdullāh was born fifteen years before the Prophet ﷺ announced his prophethood. He accepted Islam at a very young age. Prior to his acceptance, he used to herd the flocks of ʿUqbah ibn Abī Muʿayṭ. However, he later gave up this job and requested that the Prophet ﷺ allow him to stay in his service, which he ﷺ graciously accepted. While serving the Prophet ﷺ, ʿAbdullāh learnt the Qur'ān from the Prophet with a great amount of efficiency. The Prophet was so pleased by his efforts that he advised others to learn from him. *Ṣaḥīḥ al-Bukhārī* (3759). On one occasion, he even asked him to recite the Qur'ān to him. *Ṣaḥīḥ al-Bukhārī* (5049). Hudhayfah said of him, 'I do not know anyone who resembles the Prophet ﷺ more in terms of looks and conduct than Ibn Masʿūd. *Ṣaḥīḥ al-Bukhārī* (3762).

ʿAbdullāh ibn Masʿūd narrated 848 hadiths. He passed away in the year 32/652 at the age of 60.

HADITH 2

- Qutaybah ibn Saʿīd ibn Jamīl al-Thaqafī
- Abū ʿAbdillāh Jarīr ibn ʿAbd al-Ḥamīd al-Kūfī
- Ḥasan ibn ʿUbayd Allāh an-Nakhaʾī al-Kūfī
- Abū ʿAmr ash-Shaybānī Saʿd ibn Iyās al-Kūfī

ʿAbdullāh ibn Masʿūd: *see Hadith 1*

HADITH 3

- Qays ibn Ḥafṣ at-Tamīmī ad-Dārimī
- ʿAbd al-Wāḥid ibn Ziyād al-Baṣrī
- Ḥasan ibn ʿUbayd Allāh an-Nakhaʿī al-Kūfī
- Abū ʿAmr ash-Shaybānī Saʿd ibn Iyās al-Kūfī

ʿAbdullāh ibn Masʿūd: *see Hadith 1*

HADITH 4

- Abū Nuʿaym Faḍl ibn ʿAmr at-Taymī al-Qurashī
- Isrāʾīl ibn Yūnus al-Kūfī
- Abū Isḥāq ʿAmr ibn ʿAbdillah as-Sabīʿī
- Abū al-Aḥwaṣ ʿAwf ibn Malik al-Jushamī

ʿAbdullāh ibn Masʿūd: *see Hadith 1*

HADITH 5

- Muḥammad ibn Yūsuf ad-Dabbī
- Isrāʾīl ibn Yūnus al-Kūfī
- Simāk ibn Ḥarb al-Bakrī al-Kufī
- Muṣʿab ibn Saʿd al-Madanī
- Saʿd ibn Abī Waqqāṣ Malik ibn Uhayb az-Zuhrī al-Qurashī ﵁:

Saʿd was born fifteen years prior to the announcement of Prophethood and was one of the earliest Companions to accept the message of Islam, which he did at the age of seventeen. He took part in all battles with the Prophet ﷺ and was highly praised for his efforts on the battlefield. He was the first to ever shoot an arrow in the path of Allah. (*Ṣaḥīḥ al-Bukhārī* (2728), *Ṣaḥīḥ Muslim* (7433)). He was also a guard of the Prophet ﷺ when, one night, he ﷺ could not sleep and wished for someone to guard him for the night. Saʿd stepped forward and guarded the Prophet ﷺ, which eased him and allowed him to sleep peacefully. *Ṣaḥīḥ al-Bukhārī* (2885), *Ṣaḥīḥ Muslim* (6230). He was blessed to be given the glad tidings of Paradise, as narrated in the hadith *Sunan Abī Dāwūd* (4649), *Jamiʿ at-Tirmidhī* (3747).

Saʿd ibn Abī Waqqāṣ narrated 271 hadiths from the Prophet ﷺ. He passed away at the age of 72 in the year 58/677.

HADITH 6

- ʿAlī ibn ʿAbdillāh as-Saʿdī
- Sufyān ibn ʿUyaynah al-Kūfī al-Makkī
- ʿUmārah ibn al-Qaʿqāʿ ibn Shubrumah al-Kūfī
- Abū Zurʿah ibn ʿAmr al-Bajalī al-Kūfī
- Abū Hurayrah ʿAbd ar-Raḥmān ibn Ṣakhr ad-Dawsī al-Yamanī رضي الله عنه:

Better known as Abū Hurayrah (father of the kitten), he accepted Islam at the beginning of the seventh year after the migration of the Prophet ﷺ to Madīnah. He was one of the 'People of the Porch' (*Ahl aṣ-Ṣuffah*), who were very poor and spent their time in the Masjid an-Nabawī. He would try his utmost to spend as much time as he could in the company of the Prophet ﷺ. He persistently invited his mother to accept Islam, but she would always refuse. On one occasion he did so and in return she replied with ill words regarding the Prophet ﷺ. Abū Hurayrah came to the Prophet ﷺ with tears in his eyes and explained the situation. The Prophet ﷺ raised his hands in supplication for his mother. On his return home, Abū Hurayrah found his mother washing herself and, after allowing him to enter, she declared her acceptance of the message of Islam. He was delighted and cried tears of joy. *Ṣaḥīḥ Muslim* (6396).

Abū Hurayrah narrated 5374 hadiths from the Prophet ﷺ. He used to say regarding himself, 'I attended those gatherings of the Prophet ﷺ which the Emigrants (*Muhajirūn*) and Helpers (*Anṣār*) would not attend, and thus I memorised what they did not. *Ṣaḥīḥ al-Bukhārī* (118), *Ṣaḥīḥ Muslim* (6397). He passed away at the age of 78 in the year 57/676.

HADITH 7

- Qutaybah ibn Saʿīd ibn Jamīl ath-Thaqafī
- Abū ʿAbdillāh Jarīr ibn ʿAbd al-Ḥamīd al-Kūfī
- ʿUmārah ibn al-Qaʿqāʿ ibn Shubrumah al-Kūfī
- Abū Zurʿah ibn ʿAmr al-Bajalī al-Kūfī

Abū Hurayrah ؓ: *see Hadith 6*

HADITH 8

- Sulaymān ibn Ḥarb al-Baṣrī
- Wuhayb ibn Khālid al-Bāhilī
- ʿUmārah ibn al-Qaʿqāʿ ibn Shubrumah al-Kūfī
- Abū Zurʿah ibn ʿAmr al-Bajalī al-Kūfī

Abū Hurayrah ؓ: *see Hadith 6*

HADITH 9

- Muḥammad ibn Kathīr al-ʿAbdī al-Baṣrī
- Sufyān ibn ʿUyaynah al-Kūfī al-Makkī
- Ḥabīb ibn Abī Thābit al-Kūfī

- Abū 'l-ʿAbbās as-Sā'ib ibn Furūkh al-Makkī
- ʿAbdullah ibn ʿAmr ibn al-ʿĀṣ al-Qurashī ﷺ:

ʿAbdullāh ibn ʿAmr was born seven years after the announcement of Prophethood. He accepted Islam in the year 7/628 and migrated to Madīnah. He was one of the only Companions to be given permission during the Prophet's ﷺ lifetime to write down the Prophetic narrations that he heard. Abu Hurayrah ﷺ said of him, 'Nobody is more knowledgeable than me in regards to the Prophetic narrations, except for ʿAbdullah ibn ʿAmr, because he would write them down and I would memorise them.' *Ṣaḥīḥ al-Bukhārī* (113).

ʿAbdullāh ibn ʿAmr narrated 700 hadiths from the Prophet ﷺ. He passed away at the age of 72 in the year 67 AH.

HADITH 10

- Abū Nuʿaym al-Faḍl ibn ʿAmr at-Taymī al-Qurashī
- Sufyān ibn ʿUyaynah al-Kūfī al-Makkī
- ʿAṭā' ibn as-Sā'ib al-Kūfī
- Sā'ib ibn Malik al-Kūfī

ʿAbdullāh ibn ʿAmr ﷺ: *see Hadith 9*

HADITH 11

- Yaḥyā ibn ʿAbdillāh ibn Bukayr al-Miṣrī
- Layth ibn Saʿd ibn ʿAbd ar-Raḥmān al-Fahmī
- ʿUqayl ibn Khālid ibn ʿAqīl al-Aylī
- Ibn Shihāb Muḥammad ibn Muslim ibn ʿUbayd Allāh al-Qurashī az-Zuhrī
- Anas ibn Mālik ibn Naḍr al-Anṣārī ﷺ:

Anas was born in Madīnah in the third year of Prophethood and accepted Islam at a young age. After the Prophet ﷺ migrated to

Madīnah, his mother brought him to the Prophet ﷺ and said, 'This is my son. I give him to you to be your slave. The Prophet ﷺ accepted him in his service.' He ﷺ made supplication for increase in his wealth and offspring and Anas himself mentions how the supplication was accepted and that he had a lot of wealth and offspring. (*Ṣaḥīḥ al-Bukhārī* (1982), *Ṣaḥīḥ Muslim* (2480)). He said, 'A night would not go by except that I would see my beloved ﷺ.' *Aṭ-Ṭabaqāt al-Kubrā*, 7:15.

Anas narrated 2286 hadiths from the Prophet ﷺ. He passed away at the age of 103 in the year 93/711.

HADITH 12

- Muḥammad ibn Saʿīd al-Khuzāʿī al-Baṣrī
- Ḥazm ibn Abī Ḥazm al-Quṭaʿī al-Baṣrī
- Maymūn ibn Siyāh al-Baṣrī

Anas ibn Mālik ﷺ: *see Hadith 11*

HADITH 13

- Muʿādh ibn Faḍālah az-Zahrānī
- Hishām ibn Abī ʿAbdillāh Sanbar al-Baṣrī ad-Dustuwāʾī
- Yaḥyā ibn Abī Kathīr aṭ-Ṭāʾī
- Abū Jaʿfar al-Anṣārī al-Madanī

Abū Hurayrah ﷺ: *see Hadith 6*

HADITH 14

- Bishr ibn Muḥammad as-Sakhtiyānī
- ʿAbdullāh ibn al-Mubārak al-Marwazī
- Muḥammad ibn Shuʿayb ibn Shābūr al-Umawī
- ʿUmar ibn Yazīd an-Naṣrī ash-Shāmī

- Abū Sallām Mamṭūr al-Ḥabashī
- Abū Umāmah Ṣudayy ibn ʿAjlān ibn Wahb al-Bāhilī ﷺ:

Abū Umāmah was born seven years prior to the announcement of Prophethood; however, it is unknown when he accepted Islam. When the Prophet ﷺ sent him to his people to invite them to Islam, they verbally tortured him at first, but later accepted Islam. He would always try to fast (*ṣawm*), after the Prophet ﷺ advised him that there is nothing better than it. *Sunan an-Nasāʾī* (2220).

He narrated 250 hadiths from the Prophet ﷺ. He passed away at the age of 106 in the year 86/705.

HADITH 15

- Qabīṣah ibn ʿUqbah ibn Muḥammad as-Suwāʾī
- Sufyān ibn ʿUyaynah al-Kūfī al-Makkī
- Suhayl ibn Abī Ṣāliḥ al-Madanī
- Abū Suhayl Sammān Dhakwān al-Madanī

Abū Hurayrah ﷺ: *see Hadith 6*

HADITH 16

- Musaddad ibn Musarhad ibn Musarbal
- Bishr ibn al-Muffaḍḍal al-Raqāshī
- Saʿīd ibn Iyās al-Jarīrī al-Baṣrī
- ʿAbd ar-Raḥmān ibn Abī Bakrah al-Baṣrī
- Abū Bakrah Nufayʿ ibn al-Ḥārith ath-Thaqafī ﷺ:

Abu Bakrah accepted Islam at the hands of the Prophet ﷺ in the year 8/629. He was previously a slave but the Prophet ﷺ freed him. He narrated 132 hadiths from the Prophet ﷺ. He passed away in the year 51/671.

HADITH 17

- Khālid ibn Makhlad al-Qaṭawānī
- Sulaymān ibn Bilāl at-Taymī
- Suhayl ibn Abī Ṣāliḥ al-Madanī
- Abū Suhayl Sammān Dhakwān al-Madanī

Abū Hurayrah ﷺ: *see Hadith 6*

HADITH 18

- Muḥammad ibn al-Faḍl as-Sadūsī al-Baṣrī
- Abū ʿAwānah Waḍḍāḥ al-Yashkurī al-Bazzār
- Suhayl ibn Abī Ṣāliḥ al-Madanī
- Abū Suhayl Sammān Dhakwān al-Madanī

Abū Hurayrah ﷺ: *see Hadith 6*

HADITH 19

- Musaddad ibn Musarhad ibn Musarbal
- Bishr ibn al-Muffaḍḍal al-Raqāshī
- ʿAbd ar-Raḥmān ibn Isḥāq al-Madanī
- Saʿīd ibn Abī Saʿīd al-Maqburī al-Madanī

Abū Hurayrah ﷺ: *see Hadith 6*

HADITH 20

- Ibn Abī Uways Ismāʾīl ibn ʿAbdillāh al-Asbaḥī al-Madanī
- ʿAbd al-Ḥamīd ibn ʿAbdillāh al-Madanī [brother of Ibn Abī Uways]
- Sulaymān ibn Bilāl at-Taymī
- Muḥammad ibn Hilāl al-Madanī
- Saʿd ibn Isḥāq ibn Kaʿb ibn ʿUjrah as-Sālimī

- Abū Saʿd ibn Isḥāq Kaʿb ibn ʿUjrah ibn Umayyah al-Balawī al-Anṣārī as-Sālimī ﷺ:

Kaʿb ibn ʿUjrah was born three years prior to the announcement of Prophethood. His acceptance of Islam was slightly delayed, but when a dear friend of his came and broke the idol that he used to worship, he realised this so-called god was unable to defend itself, so he accepted Islam. He took part in all the Battles with the Prophet ﷺ. He said regarding the verse of the Qur'an (2:196) in which Allah made an exception for those unable to shave their head after Hajj (or *ʿumrah*) that it was revealed especially for him. *Ṣaḥīḥ al-Bukhārī* (4517), *Ṣaḥīḥ Muslim* (2734).

Kaʿb narrated 47 hadiths from the Prophet ﷺ. He passed away at the age of 77 in the year 51/672.

HADITH 21

- ʿAbdullāh ibn Ṣāliḥ ibn Muslim al-ʿIjlī
- Layth ibn Saʿd ibn ʿAbd ar-Raḥmān al-Fahmī
- Ibrāhīm ibn Aʿyan ash-Shaybānī al-Baṣrī
- Ḥakam ibn Abān al-ʿAdanī
- ʿIkrimah (the servant of Ibn ʿAbbās)
- ʿAbdullāh ibn al-ʿAbbās ibn ʿAbd al-Muṭṭalib ﷺ:

Ibn ʿAbbās was born three years prior to the migration of the Prophet ﷺ to Madīnah. His mother was Umm al-Faḍl Lubābah bint al-Ḥārith, who was the second female to convert to Islam. His mother brought him to the Prophet ﷺ when he was born and he ﷺ put some of his saliva on his tongue. He was very dear and close to the Prophet ﷺ and spent the majority of his life in his service. He was only thirteen years old when the Prophet ﷺ passed away. The Prophet ﷺ made supplication for him to be given knowledge of the Qur'an (*Ṣaḥīḥ al-Bukhārī* (75)) and become a learned scholar in religious matters. (*Ṣaḥīḥ al-Bukhārī* (143), *Ṣaḥīḥ Muslim* (6368)).

Ibn ʿAbbās narrated 1660 hadiths from the Prophet ﷺ. He was highly regarded amongst the Companions of the Prophet ﷺ and they would regularly seek his advice in religious matters. He passed away at the age of 71 in the year 68/687.

HADITH 22

- ʿAbdullāh ibn Yazīd al-Makkī
- Ḥaywah ibn Shurayḥ at-Tujībī
- Abū ʿUthmān Walīd ibn Abī 'l-Walīd al-Madanī
- ʿAbdullāh ibn Dīnār al-ʿAdawī al-Madanī
- ʿAbdullāh ibn ʿUmar ibn al-Khaṭṭāb al-Qurashī ؓ:

ʿAbdullāh was born in the year of Prophethood and accepted Islam at the age of six. He migrated to Madīnah and spent his time with his father in the company of the Prophet ﷺ.

He was too young to participate in the Battles of Badr and Uḥud, but took part in the battles thereafter. He was very close to the Prophet ﷺ and would try to imitate him in all his actions. He would pray in every possible location he knew that the Prophet ﷺ had prayed in, sit where he knew the Prophet ﷺ had sat and even water the tree where he knew the Prophet ﷺ had sat in the shade. ʿĀ'ishah ؓ used to say that nobody followed the footsteps of the Prophet ﷺ more than Ibn ʿUmar. *Aṭ-Ṭabaqāt al-Kubrā*, 4:108.

ʿAbdullāh narrated 2630 hadiths from the Prophet ﷺ and he is said to have been very careful in narrating from him ﷺ. The Companions would seek legal verdicts (*fatāwā*) from him. He passed away in Makkah at the age of 86 in the year 73/692.

HADITH 23

- ʿAlī ibn ʿAbdillāh ibn Jaʿfar as-Saʿdī
- Anas ibn ʿIyāḍ al-Laythī

- ʿAbdullāh ibn Yazīd ibn Qusayṭ
- Abū ʿAbdillāh Yazīd ibn Qusayṭ
- Saʿīd ibn al-Musayyib ibn Ḥazn al-Qurashī al-Makhzūmī

Abū Hurayrah ﷺ: *see Hadith 6*

HADITH 24

- Abū' l-Walīd Hishām ibn ʿAbd al-Malik al-Bāhilī aṭ-Ṭiyālisī
- Abū Bisṭām Shuʿbah ibn al-Hajjāj al-Azdī
- Sufyān ibn Ḥusayn ibn Ḥasan al-Wāsiṭī
- Muḥammad ibn Muslim ibn ʿUbayd Allāh al-Qurashī az-Zuhrī
- Muḥammad ibn Jubayr ibn Muṭʿim al-Qurashī
- Abū Muḥammad Jubayr ibn Muṭʿim ibn ʿAdī al-Qurashī ﷺ:

It is not known when Jubayr was born. The Prophet ﷺ desired for him to accept Islam (*Al-Mustadrak ʿalā aṣ-Ṣaḥīḥayn* (6685)) and he did so at the Conquest of Makkah. He was known for his knowledge of genealogy.

Jubayr narrated 60 hadiths from the Prophet ﷺ. He passed away in the year 57/676.

HADITH 25

- ʿAbdullāh ibn Ṣāliḥ ibn Muslim al-ʿIjlī
- Layth ibn Saʿd ibn ʿAbd ar-Raḥmān al-Fahmī
- ʿUqayl ibn Khālid ibn ʿAqīl al-Aylī
- Ibn Shihāb Muḥammad ibn Muslim ibn ʿUbayd Allāh al-Qurashī az-Zuhrī

Anas ibn Mālik ﷺ: *see Hadith 11*

HADITH 26

- Ḥajjāj ibn Minhāl al-Baṣrī
- Abū Bisṭām Shuʿbah ibn al-Hajjāj al-Azdī
- Muḥammad ibn ʿAbd al-Jabbār al-Anṣārī
- Muḥammad ibn Kaʿb al-Quraẓī al-Madanī

Abū Hurayrah ﷺ: *see Hadith 6*

HADITH 27

- Sulaymān ibn ʿAbd ar-Raḥmān at-Tamīmī
- Sulaymān ibn ʿUtbah al-Akhnas
- Yūnus ibn Maysarah ibn Ḥalbas
- Abū Idrīs ʿĀ'idh ibn ʿAbdillāh al-Khawlāni
- Abū ad-Dardā' ʿUwaymir ibn Zayd ibn Qays al-Anṣārī ﷺ:

Abū ad-Dardā' was born 27 years prior to the announcement of Prophethood. He accepted Islam on the day of the Battle of Badr. The Prophet ﷺ referred to him as an excellent horse rider in the battle of Uḥud. (*Al-Mustadrak ʿalā aṣ-Ṣaḥīḥayn* (5547)). He was a highly regarded Companion of the Prophet ﷺ, who memorised the Holy Qur'an and recited it to the Prophet ﷺ. He was sent to Damascus by ʿUmar ibn al-Khaṭṭāb and was the first person to be appointed as a judge in Damascus. He was a very pious person, would fast regularly and spent most of his night in prayer, until Salmān al-Fārisī advised him to spend time with his family and also give some rest to his body. *Ṣaḥīḥ al-Bukhārī* (1968).

Abū ad-Dardā' narrated 179 hadiths from the Prophet ﷺ. He passed away at the age of 72 in the year 32/652.

HADITH 28

- Qays ibn Hafṣ at-Tamīmī ad-Dārimī
- ʿAbd al-Wāḥid ibn Ziyād al-Baṣrī

- Ḥasan ibn ʿAmr al-Fuqaymī
- Mujāhid ibn Jabr al-Makhzūmī al-Makkī

ʿAbdullāh ibn ʿAmr ﵁: *see Hadith 9*

HADITH 29

- Saʿīd ibn Abī Maryam al-Ḥakam ibn Muḥammad al-Jumahī
- Sulaymān ibn Bilāl al-Taymī
- Muʿāwiyah ibn Abī Muzarrid al-Madanī
- Yazīd ibn Rūmān al-Madanī
- ʿUrwah ibn az-Zubayr ibn al-ʿAwwām al-Asadī
- ʿĀʾishah bint Abī Bakr aṣ-Ṣiddīq ibn ʿUthmān at-Taymī ﵂:

ʿĀʾishah ﵂, wife of the Prophet ﷺ and Mother of the Believers, was also known as Umm ʿAbdillāh. She was born into a blessed family five years after the announcement of Prophethood. Her father was Abū Bakr aṣ-Ṣiddīq ﵁ and her mother Umm Rūmān Zaynab bint ʿĀmir al-Kināniyyah, regarding whom the Messenger of Allah ﷺ said: 'Whoever wants to see a Woman of Jannah, they should look at Umm Rūmān.' *Aṭ-Ṭabaqāt al-Kubrā*, 8:216.

ʿĀʾishah was very dear to the Prophet ﷺ. On one occasion, he ﷺ was asked who was the most beloved person to him? He replied: "ʿĀʾishah.' *Ṣaḥīḥ al-Bukhārī* (3662), *Ṣaḥīḥ Muslim* (6177). She was known to be among the most knowledgeable of the Companions of the Prophet ﷺ and narrated 2210 hadiths from him. She departed from this world on Tuesday 17th of Ramadan 58/678, at the age of 66, and was buried in Baqīʿ al-Gharqad.

HADITH 30

- ʿUbayd Allāh ibn Mūsā ibn Bādham al-ʿAbsī al-Kūfī
- Abū Idām Sulaymān ibn Zayd al-Muḥāribī al-Kūfī
- ʿAbdullāh ibn Abī Awfā Khālid ibn ʿAlqamah al-Aslamī ﵁:

ʿAbdullāh ibn Abī Awfā was born a year before the announcement of Prophethood.

It is not clear when he accepted Islam, but he took part in seven battles with the Prophet ﷺ. *Ṣaḥīḥ al-Bukhārī* (5495), *Ṣaḥīḥ Muslim* (5045). He stayed in Madīnah until the death of the Prophet ﷺ and thereafter moved to Kufah. He passed away at the age of 100 in the year 86/705.

HADITH 31

- ʿAbdullāh ibn Ṣāliḥ ibn Muslim al-ʿIjlī
- Layth ibn Saʿd ibn ʿAbd ar-Raḥmān al-Fahmī
- ʿUqayl ibn Khālid ibn ʿAqīl al-Aylī
- Ibn Shihāb Muḥammad ibn Muslim ibn ʿUbayd Allāh al-Qurashī az-Zuhrī
- Muḥammad ibn Jubayr ibn Muṭʿim al-Qurashī

Abū Muḥammad Jubayr ibn Muṭʿim ﵁: *see Hadith 24*

HADITH 32

- Ḥafṣ ibn ʿUmar an-Namirī
- Abū Bisṭām Shuʿbah ibn al-Hajjāj al-Azdī
- Muḥammad ibn ʿAbd al-Jabbār al-Anṣārī
- Muḥammad ibn Kaʿb al-Quraẓī al-Madanī

Abū Hurayrah ﵁: *see Hadith 6*

HADITH 33

- ʿAlī ibn ʿAbdillāh as-Saʿdī
- Sufyān ibn ʿUyaynah al-Kūfī al-Makkī
- Ibrāhīm ibn Yazīd ibn Sharīk at-Taymī al-Kūfī: *see Commentary*

HADITH 34

- Abū Nuʿaym Faḍl ibn ʿAmr at-Taymī al-Qurashī
- Sufyān ibn ʿUyaynah al-Kūfī al-Makkī
- Abū Ḥayyān Yaḥyā ibn Saʿīd ibn Ḥayyān at-Taymī
- Ibrāhīm ibn Yazīd ibn Sharīk at-Taymī al-Kūfī: *see Commentary*

HADITH 35

- Abū 'l-Ḥasan Ādam ibn Abī Iyās al-Khurāsānī
- Abū Bisṭām Shuʿbah ibn al-Hajjāj al-Azdī
- ʿAmr ibn Dīnār al-Makkī
- Jābir ibn ʿAbdillāh al-Anṣārī ﷺ:

Jābir was born in the city of Madīnah (formerly known as Yathrib) 3 years before the announcement of Prophethood and accepted Islam at the age of nine before the migration of the Prophet ﷺ to Madīnah. His father was among those Companions who participated in the battle of Badr and was martyred in the battle of Uḥud. He himself was keen on partaking in those battles; however, he had sisters whom his father had left him behind to look after. He became a close Companion of the Prophet ﷺ and took part in 19 battles further with him. During preparation for the Battle of the Trench, he was involved in an extraordinary event, (*Ṣaḥīḥ al-Bukhārī* (4101), *Ṣaḥīḥ Muslim* (5315)) whereby the Companions, who had not eaten for three days, ate from a young she-goat and some bread that he owned and it sufficed the whole army.

Jābir narrated 1540 hadiths from the Prophet ﷺ and people would come to him to learn the hadiths of the Prophet ﷺ. He passed away at the age of 98 in the year 78/697.

HADITH 36

- Sufyān ibn ʿUyaynah al-Kūfī al-Makkī
- Hadith 37
- Aḥmad ibn Ḥumayd aṭ-Ṭuraythīthī
- Abū Bakr ibn ʿAyyāsh al-Kūfī
- Abū Ḥaṣīn ʿUthmān ibn ʿAṣim al-Kūfī
- Abū Ṣāliḥ Sammān Dhakwān al-Madanī

Abū Hurayrah ﷺ: *see Hadith 6*

HADITH 38

- Musaddad ibn Musarhad ibn Musarbal
- Abū al-Aḥwaṣ ʿAwf ibn Malik al-Jushamī
- Saʿīd ibn Masrūq ath-Thawrī
- Abū Ḥāzim Salmān al-Ashjaʿī al-Kūfī

Abū Hurayrah ﷺ: *see Hadith 6*

HADITH 39

- Faḍl ibn al-Muqātil al-Azdī al-Balkhī
- ʿAbdullāh ibn Ibrāhīm aṣ-Ṣanʿānī
- Abū ʿAbdillāh Ibrāhīm ibn ʿUmar ibn Kaysān aṣ-Ṣanʿānī
- ʿAbdullāh ibn Abī Najīḥ al-Makkī

HADITH 40

- Muḥammad ibn Salām al-Bukhārī
- Sufyān ibn ʿUyaynah al-Kūfī al-Makkī

HADITH 41

- Abū ʿAbdillāh al-Musnadī Muḥammad ibn ʿAbdillāh ibn Jaʿfar al-Bukhārī
- Salm ibn Sālim al-Balkhī
- Sufyān ibn ʿUyaynah al-Kūfī al-Makkī

HADITH 42

- Ibrāhīm ibn Mūsā at-Tamīmī
- Ibn Abī Zā'idah Yaḥyā ibn Zakariyyā al-Hamdānī al-Wādi'ī
- Zakariyyā ibn Abī Zā'idah
- Khālid ibn Salamah al-Makhzūmī al-Kūfī
- ʿAbdullāh al-Bahī (servant of Muṣʿab ibn az-Zubayr)
- ʿUrwah ibn az-Zubayr ibn al-ʿAwwām al-Asadī

ʿĀ'ishah bint Abī Bakr aṣ-Ṣiddīq ﵂: *see Hadith 29*

HADITH 43

- Musaddad ibn Musarhad ibn Musarbal
- Yaḥyā ibn Saʿīd ibn Farrūkh at-Tamīmī
- Thawr ibn Yazīd al-Ḥimṣī
- Ḥabīb ibn ʿUbayd ar-Raḥabī al-Ḥimṣī
- Miqdām ibn Maʿdī Karib ibn ʿAmr al-Kindī ﵁:

Miqdām was born nine years after the announcement of Prophethood and accepted Islam at a young age. The Prophet ﷺ gave him glad tidings of being successful if he avoided taking up a position of authority. *Sunan Abī Dāwūd* (2933).

He narrated 40 hadiths from the Prophet ﷺ. He passed away at the age of 91 in the year 87/705.

HADITH 44

- Musā ibn Ismāʿīl al-Minqarī
- Abū ʿĀṣim aḍ-Ḍaḥḥāk ibn Makhlad ibn aḍ-Ḍaḥḥāk ash-Shaybānī al-Baṣrī

HADITH 45

- Musaddad ibn Musarhad ibn Musarbal
- Ismāʿīl ibn Ibrāhīm al-Asadī al-Kūfī
- Ziyād ibn Mikhrāq al-Baṣrī
- Muʿāwiyah ibn Qurrah al-Muzanī al-Baṣrī
- Abū Muʿāwiyah Qurrah ibn Iyās al-Muzanī ﷺ:

Not much is known about his birth or acceptance of Islam. There is an incident recorded in which he says he visited the Prophet ﷺ and asked to see the stamp of prophethood, so the Prophet ﷺ told him to put his hand on his back. He narrates that he saw it between the Prophet's ﷺ shoulders, shaped like an egg. *Sunan an-Nasāʾī al-Kubrā* (8249), *Musnad aṭ-Ṭayālisī* (1167). He also mentions that during the lifetime of the Prophet ﷺ he would only have dates and water as his meals. (*Musnad al-Bazzār* (3307)). He took part in the Battle of the Trench.

He narrated approximately 25 hadiths from the Prophet ﷺ and is one of the 26 Companions who narrated the story of the Mahdī (Messiah) from the Prophet ﷺ. *ʿAqīdat Ahl as-Sunnah wa 'l-Athar fī 'l-Mahdī al-Muntaẓar*, p. 128. He passed away in the year 64/683.

HADITH 46

- Ibrāhīm ibn al-Mundhir al-Asadī al-Ḥizāmī
- Maʿn ibn ʿĪsā al-Ashjaʿī al-Madanī
- Muʿāwiyah ibn Ṣāliḥ al-Ḥaḍramī
- ʿAbd ar-Raḥmān ibn Jubayr al-Ḥaḍramī

- Abū ʿAbd ar-Raḥmān Jubayr ibn Nufayr al-Ḥaḍramī
- Nawwās ibn Samʿān al-Anṣārī al-Kilābī ﷺ:

It is not known when Nawwās was born or when he accepted Islam. His father was part of a delegation that came to the Prophet ﷺ and learned part of the Holy Qur'an from him.

He narrated very few hadiths from the Prophet ﷺ, among them the story of Dajjāl (the Anti-Christ) and the description of him. *Ṣaḥīḥ Muslim* (7373).

HADITH 47

- Abū 'l-Yamān Ḥakam ibn Nāfiʿ al-Bahrānī
- Shuʿayb ibn Abī Ḥamzah al-Umawī al-Ḥimṣī
- Ibn Shihāb Muḥammad ibn Muslim ibn ʿUbayd Allāh al-Qurashī az-Zuhrī
- Sālim ibn ʿAbdillāh ibn ʿUmar ibn al-Khaṭṭāb al-Qurashī al-Madanī

Abū Sālim ʿAbdullāh ibn ʿUmar ﷺ: *See Hadith 22*

HADITH 48

- ʿAbdullāh ibn az-Zubayr al-Ḥumaydī
- Sufyān ibn ʿUyaynah al-Kūfī al-Makkī
- Muḥammad ibn ʿAmr ibn ʿAlqamah
- Yaḥyā ibn ʿAbd ar-Raḥmān ibn Ḥāṭib al-Madanī
- ʿAbdullāh ibn az-Zubayr ibn al-ʿAwwām al-Qurashī ﷺ
- Zubayr ibn al-ʿAwwām ibn Khuwaylid al-Qurashī ﷺ:

Zubayr was born twelve years prior to the announcement of Prophethood. His mother was very strict with him. When asked the reason, she said, 'So that he may become strong and intelligent in his life.' He accepted Islam through the efforts of Abū Bakr ﷺ at the age of eight. He was known as a brave fighter and participated in all the battles with the Prophet ﷺ. He would say that the Prophet ﷺ never left for a battle without him being there. *Al-Mustadrak ʿalā aṣ-Ṣaḥīḥayn* (5657) He was one of only two men riding a horse in the Battle of Badr, in which he wore a yellow turban on his head. The angels descended to assist the Muslims in this battle and they were all wearing yellow turbans. According to ʿAlī ﷺ, the Prophet ﷺ described Zubayr as his neighbour in Jannah.

Zubayr narrated 38 hadiths from the Prophet ﷺ. When asked why he narrated so few hadith, he replied that he feared the saying of the Prophet ﷺ: 'Whoever ascribes to me something I have not said, let him take his seat in Hell-fire.' *Ṣaḥīḥ al-Bukhārī* (109). He passed away at the age of 61 in the year 36/656.

HADITH 49

- Abū Thābit Muḥammad ibn ʿUbayd Allah ibn Muḥammad al-Madanī
- ʿUmar ibn Ṭalḥah ibn ʿAlqamah al-Waqqāṣī al-Madani
- Muḥammad ibn ʿAmr ibn ʿAlqamah
- Yaḥyā ibn ʿAbd ar-Raḥmān ibn Ḥāṭib al-Madanī
- ʿAbdullāh ibn az-Zubayr ibn al-ʿAwwām al-Qurashī ﷺ:

ʿAbdullāh was the first Muslim child to be born to the Emigrants (*Muhājirūn*) in the first year after Migration. His mother was Asmāʾ, daughter of the great Companion Abū Bakr ﷺ.

His mother narrates that when he was born, he was brought to the Prophet ﷺ, who chewed on a date and placed it in ʿAbdullāh's mouth (known as '*taḥnīk*'). Thus, the saliva of the Prophet ﷺ was the first thing to enter his stomach. *Ṣaḥīḥ al-Bukhārī* (3909), *Ṣaḥīḥ Muslim* (5616).

He was highly respected amongst the Companions and on one occasion, when Ibn ʿAbbās ﷺ was asked about him, he said: 'His father [Zubayr ﷺ] was the disciple of the Prophet ﷺ; his maternal grandfather [Abu Bakr ﷺ] was the companion in the cave; his mother

[Asmā' ﷺ] was the one who tore her belt to tie the provisions for the Prophet ﷺ on his journey from Makkah to Madīnah; his aunt [ʿĀ'ishah ﷺ] is the Mother of the Believers; his paternal aunt [Khadījah] was the first wife of the Prophet ﷺ; and his grandmother [Ṣafiyyah ﷺ] was the paternal aunt of the Prophet ﷺ. He himself is very pure and righteous and he is a reciter of the Holy Qur'an.' *Ṣaḥīḥ al-Bukhārī* (4665).

He narrated 33 hadiths from the Prophet ﷺ. He was very knowledgeable in regards to the laws pertaining to Hajj. He passed away at the age of 72 in the year 73/692.

HADITH 50

- Sulaymān ibn Dāwūd al-Maṣrī
- Yaʿqūb ibn ʿAbdillāh al-Ashʿarī al-Qummī
- Jaʿfar ibn Abī 'l-Mughīrah al-Khuzāʿī al-Qummī
- Saʿīd ibn Jubayr ibn Hishām al-Asadī

ʿAbdullāh ibn ʿUmar ﷺ: *See Hadith 22*

HADITH 51

- Muḥammad ibn Kathīr al-ʿAbdī al-Baṣrī
- Sulaymān ibn Kathīr al-ʿAbdī al-Baṣrī
- Muḥammad ibn Muslim ibn ʿUbayd Allāh al-Qurashī az-Zuhrī
- ʿUrwah ibn az-Zubayr ibn al-ʿAwwām al-Asadī
- Usāmah ibn Zayd ibn Ḥārithah ﷺ:

Usāmah was born five years after the announcement of Prophethood. His parents, Zayd ibn Ḥārithah and Umm Ayman ﷺ, were both very dear to the Prophet ﷺ and accepted Islam at an early stage; thus, he grew up in an Islamic environment. The Prophet ﷺ had adopted him as his son and he was very beloved to him. On one occasion, he ﷺ held his grandson, Ḥasan ﷺ, and Usāmah, and said: 'O Allah, love them, for indeed I love them.' *Ṣaḥīḥ al-Bukhārī* (3735).

Usāmah was known for his bravery and desire to take part in battles with the Prophet ﷺ, although his father refused, due to his age. In the Battle of Uḥud, he entered the battlefield carrying a sword that was taller than him. When his father saw him he advised him to go back. At the age of seventeen, he was appointed by the Prophet ﷺ as a general to an army that included Abū Bakr and ʿUmar ﷺ.

He narrated 128 hadiths from the Prophet ﷺ. He passed away at the age of 61 in the year 54/673.

HADITH 52

- Faḍl ibn Dukayn al-Kūfī at-Taymī
- Sufyān ibn ʿUyaynah al-Kūfī al-Makkī
- Muḥammad ibn Muslim ibn ʿUbayd Allāh al-Qurashī az-Zuhrī
- ʿUrwah ibn az-Zubayr ibn al-ʿAwwām al-Asadī

Usāmah ibn Zayd ﷺ: *see Hadith 51*

HADITH 53

- ʿAbdān ʿAbdullāh ibn Aḥmad ibn Mūsā al-Ahwāzī
- ʿAbdullāh ibn al-Mubārak al-Marwazī
- Maʿmar ibn Rāshid al-Azdī al-Baṣrī
- Muḥammad ibn Muslim ibn ʿUbayd Allāh al-Qurashī az-Zuhrī
- ʿUrwah ibn az-Zubayr ibn al-ʿAwwām al-Asadī
- Kurz ibn ʿAlqamah ibn Hilāl al-Khuzāʿī ﷺ:

He accepted Islam on the day of the Conquest of Makkah. When the Prophet ﷺ and Abū Bakr ﷺ migrated from Makkah and took cover in the cave, it was he who saw the footprints near the cave, but after seeing the spiderweb around the cave, he thought they could not have entered there. He mentions that the footprints of the Prophet Muḥammad ﷺ matched those of Prophet Ibrāhīm ﷺ.

During the Caliphate of Muʿāwiyah, he was appointed to place markings on the original boundary of the Ḥaram, as he had knowledge of this. It is not known when he passed away, except that he lived a long life.

HADITH 54

- ʿAbdullāh ibn Ṣāliḥ ibn Muslim al-ʿIjlī
- Layth ibn Saʿd ibn ʿAbd ar-Raḥmān al-Fahmī
- Nāfiʿ ibn Jirjis al-Qurashī (servant of ʿAbdullāh ibn ʿUmar)

ʿAbdullāh ibn ʿUmar ﷺ: *See Hadith 22*

HADITH 55

- Abū ʾl-Ḥasan Ādam ibn Abī Iyās al-Khurāsānī
- Abū Bisṭām Shuʿbah ibn al-Hajjāj al-Azdī
- ʿUyaynah ibn ʿAbd ar-Raḥmān al-Ghaṭafānī
- Abū ʿUyaynah ibn ʿAbd ar-Raḥmān ibn Jawshan al-Ghaṭafānī

Abū Bakrah Nufayʿ ibn al-Ḥārith ﷺ: *see Hadith 16*

HADITH 56

- Umayyah ibn Bisṭām al-ʿAyshī al-Baṣrī
- Yazīd ibn Zurayʿ al-Baṣrī
- ʿAlāʾ ibn ʿAbd ar-Raḥmān al-Madanī
- ʿAbd ar-Raḥmān ibn Yaʿūqub al-Juhanī al-Madanī

Abū Hurayrah ﷺ: *see Hadith 6*

HADITH 57

- Muḥammad ibn Kathīr al-ʿAbdī al-Baṣrī
- Sufyān ibn ʿUyaynah al-Kūfī al-Makkī

- Aʿmash Sulaymān ibn Mihrān al-Asadī al-Kūfī
- Ḥasan ibn ʿAmr al-Fuqaymī
- Fiṭr ibn Khalīfah al-Kūfī al-Makhzūmī
- Mujāhid ibn Jabr al-Makhzūmī al-Makkī

ʿAbdullāh ibn ʿAmr ﷺ: *see Hadith 9*

HADITH 58

- Mālik ibn Ismāʿīl an-Nahdī al-Kūfī
- ʿĪsā ibn ʿAbd ar-Raḥmān as-Sulamī
- Ṭalhah ibn Muṣarrif al-Yāmi al-Kūfī
- ʿAbd ar-Raḥmān ibn ʿAwsajah al-Hamdānī
- Barā' ibn ʿĀzib ibn al-Ḥārith al-Anṣārī ﷺ:

Barā' was born five years after the announcement of Prophethood and accepted Islam at a young age. He was too young to participate in the Battles of Badr and Uḥud but took part in fifteen battles with the Prophet ﷺ thereafter.

He narrated 305 hadiths from the Prophet ﷺ. He passed away at the age of 80 in the year 72/691.

HADITH 59

- Abū 'l-Yamān Ḥakam ibn Nāfiʿ al-Bahrānī
- Shuʿayb ibn Abī Ḥamzah al-Umawī al-Ḥimṣī
- Muḥammad ibn Muslim ibn ʿUbayd Allāh al-Qurashī az-Zuhrī
- ʿUrwah ibn az-Zubayr ibn al-ʿAwwām al-Asadī
- Ḥakīm ibn Ḥizām ibn Khuwaylid al-Qurashī ﷺ:

Ḥakīm was born prior to the birth of the Prophet ﷺ by thirteen years. He accepted Islam ten years after the Migration of the Prophet ﷺ to Madīnah. He was the nephew of the Wife of the Prophet ﷺ, Khadījah

ﷺ. He would say that Muhammad ﷺ was the most beloved person to him. *Musnad Aḥmad* (15323).

Ḥakīm narrated 40 hadiths from the Prophet ﷺ. He passed away at the age of 120 in the year 54/673.

HADITH 60

- ʿAbd ar-Raḥmān ibn Sharīk an-Nakhaʿī
- Abū ʿAbd ar-Raḥmān Sharīk ibn ʿAbdīllāh an-Nakhaʿī al-Kūfī
- Muḥammad ibn Isḥāq ibn Yasār al-Madanī
- Bukayr ibn ʿAbdillāh al-Ashajj
- Sulaymān ibn Yasār al-Madanī (servant of Maymūnah)
- Maymūnah bint al-Ḥārith ibn Ḥazn al-Hilāliyyah ﷺ:

Maymūnah was born fifteen years before the announcement of Prophethood. It is not known when she accepted Islam. She was married to the Prophet ﷺ in the year 7/628 and is therefore called Umm al-Mu'minīn (Mother of the Believers). She was known to be a very pious and knowledgeable woman and would keep good ties with her relatives. The Prophet ﷺ testified to her faith when he ﷺ referred to her as a '*mu'minah*' ([true] believer). *Al-Mustadrak ʿalā aṣ-Ṣaḥīḥayn* (6989).

She narrated thirteen hadiths from the Prophet ﷺ. She passed away in the same place she wedded the Prophet ﷺ, at the age of 80, in the year 51/671.

HADITH 61

- Bishr ibn Muḥammad as-Sakhtiyānī
- ʿAbdullāh ibn al-Mubārak al-Marwazī
- Muʿāwiyah ibn Abī Muzarrid al-Madanī
- Saʿīd ibn Yasār al-Madanī

Abū Hurayrah ﷺ: *see Hadith 6*

HADITH 62

- 'Abdullah ibn Yusuf al-Tinisi al-Kala'i
- Layth ibn Saʿd ibn ʿAbd ar-Raḥmān al-Fahmī
- ʿUqayl ibn Khālid ibn ʿAqīl al-Aylī
- Ibn Shihāb Muḥammad ibn Muslim ibn ʿUbayd Allāh al-Qurashī az-Zuhrī
- ʿUrwah ibn az-Zubayr ibn al-ʿAwwām al-Asadī

ʿĀ'ishah bint Abī Bakr aṣ-Ṣiddīq ﷺ: *see Hadith 29*

HADITH 63

- Sulaymān ibn ʿAbd ar-Raḥmān at-Tamīmī
- Walīd ibn Muslim al-Qurashī
- ʿAbdullāh ibn al-ʿAlā' ad-Dimashqī
- Bilāl ibn Saʿd ad-Dimashqī
- Saʿd ibn Tamīm as-Sakunī al-Ashʿarī ﷺ:

There is not much known about his birth or acceptance of Islam. He was known as the Imam and Reciter (*Qāri'*) of Damascus. He narrated three hadiths from the Prophet ﷺ.

HADITH 64

- Qutaybah ibn Saʿīd ibn Jamīl ath-Thaqafī
- Layth ibn Saʿd ibn ʿAbd ar-Raḥmān al-Fahmī
- Abū az-Zubayr Muḥammad ibn Muslim al-Qurashī al-Makkī

Jābir ibn ʿAbdillāh ﷺ: *see Hadith 35*

HADITH 65

- Abū 'l-Ḥasan Ādam ibn Abī Iyās al-Khurāsānī
- Abū Bisṭām Shuʿbah ibn al-Hajjāj al-Azdī

- Ibn Abī Dhi'b Muḥammad ibn ʿAbd ar-Raḥmān al-Qurashī al-Madanī
- Saʿīd ibn Samʿān al-Anṣārī al-Zuraqī

Abū Hurayrah ﷺ: *see Hadith 6*

HADITH 66

- Muḥammad ibn ʿAbd al-Wāḥid ibn ʿAnbasah al-Qurashī
- ʿAnbasah ibn ʿAbd al-Wāḥid al-Umawī
- Bayān ibn Bishr al-Aḥmasī al-Kūfī
- Qays ibn Abī Ḥāzim al-Kufī
- ʿAmr ibn al-ʿĀṣ ibn Wā'il al-Qurashī ﷺ:

ʿAmr was born 34 years prior to the announcement of Prophethood. He accepted Islam in the year 8/629. The Prophet ﷺ was delighted with his acceptance of Islam, gave testimony to his sincerity (*Jāmiʿ at-Tirmidhī* (4179)) and called him a '*mu'min*' ([true] believer). He ﷺ also mentioned that he is from amongst the righteous of Quraysh. *Jāmiʿ at-Tirmidhī* (4180). He was appointed General by the Prophet ﷺ in the Battle of the Chains (*Maʿrakah Dhat al-Salasil*). He was renowned for his far-sightedness and bravery.

He narrated 39 hadiths from the Prophet ﷺ. He passed away at the age of 90 in the year 43/663.

HADITH 67

- Abū 'l-Ḥasan Ādam ibn Abī Iyās al-Khurāsānī
- Abū Bisṭām Shuʿbah ibn al-Hajjāj al-Azdī
- Sulayman ibn Ṭarkhān at-Taymī al-Baṣrī
- Abū ʿUthmān an-Nahdī ʿAbd ar-Raḥmān ibn Mull al-Quḍāʿī an-Nahdī

Usāmah ibn Zayd ﷺ: *see Hadith 51*

Bibliography

Abū Dāwūd, Sulaymān ibn al-Ashʿath as-Sijistānī. *Sunan Abī Dāwūd*. Beirut: Dār al-Fikr, n.d.

Aṣbahānī, Abū Nuʿaym. *Ḥilyat al-Awliyāʾ wa Ṭabaqāt al-Aṣfiyāʾ*. Beirut: Dār al-Kitāb al-ʿArabī, 1405/1985.

Aṣbahānī, Abū ʾl-Qāsīm Qawwām as-Sunnah. *At-Targhīb wa ʾt-Tarhīb*. Cairo: Dār al-Ḥadīth, 1414/1993.

Aṣbahānī, Abū ash-Shaykh. *At-Tawbīkh waʾ t-Tanbīh*. Cairo: Maktabat al-Furqān, n.d.

ʿAsqalānī, Aḥmad ibn ʿAlī ibn Ḥajar. *Fatḥ al-Bārī Sharḥ Ṣaḥīḥ al-Bukhārī*. Beirut: Dār al-Maʿrifah, 1379/1959.

Aurangzeb, Muḥammad. *Al-Fatāwā al-Hindiyyah*. Beirut: Dār al-Fikr, 1310/1892.

ʿAynī, Badr ad-Dīn. *ʿUmdat al-Qārī Sharḥ Ṣaḥīḥ al-Bukhārī*. Beirut: Dār Iḥyāʾ at-Turāth al-ʿArabī, n.d.

Baghawī, Ḥusayn ibn Masʿūd. *Sharḥ as-Sunnah*. Beirut: Al-Maktab al-Islāmī, 1403/1983.

Bayhaqī, Abū Bakr ibn al-Ḥasan ibn ʿAlī. *Al-Qaḍāʾ waʾl-Qadar*. Riyad: Maktabat al-ʿUbaykān, 1421/2000.

Bayhaqī, Abū Bakr ibn al-Ḥasan ibn ʿAlī. *Shuʿab al-Īmān*. Riyad: Maktabat ar-Rushd, 1423/2003.

Bazzār, Abū Bakr Aḥmad ibn ʿAmr ibn ʿAbd al-Khāliq. *Musnad al-Bazzār*. Madīnah: Maktabat al-ʿUlūm wa ʾl-Ḥikam, 1988–2009.

Bukhārī, Muḥammad ibn Ismāʿīl. *Al-Adab al-Mufrad*. Beirut: Dār al-Bashāʾir al-Islāmiyyah, 1409/1989.

Bukhārī, Muḥammad ibn Ismāʿīl. *Birr al-Wālidayn*. Tangier: Dār al-Ḥadīth al-Kattāniyyah, 1435/2014.

Bukhārī, Muḥammad ibn Ismāʿīl. *Khalq Afʿāl al-ʿIbād*. Riyad: Dār Aṭlas al-Khaḍrāʾ, 1425/2005.

Bukhārī, Muḥammad ibn Ismāʿīl. *Ṣaḥīḥ al-Bukhārī*. Beirut: Dār Ṭawq an-Najāh, 1422/2001.

Bukhārī, Muḥammad ibn Ismāʿīl. *At-Tārīkh al-Awsaṭ*. Riyad: Dār ar-Rushd, 1426/2005.

Bukhārī, Muḥammad ibn Ismāʿīl. *At-Tārīkh al-Kabīr*. Beirut: Dār al-Fikr, n.d.

Dehlawī, Walī Allāh Aḥmad ibn ʿAbd ar-Raḥīm. *Ḥujjat Allah al-Bālighah*. Beirut: Dār al-Jīl, 1426/2005.

Dhahabī, Shams ad-Dīn. *Mīzān al-Iʿtidāl*. Beirut: Dār al-Maʿrifah, 1382 /1963.

Dhahabī, Shams ad-Dīn. *Al-Mughnī fī ad-Duʿafāʾ*. Qatar: Idārat Iḥyāʾ at-Turāth, n.d.

Dhahabī, Shams ad-Dīn. *Siyar Aʿlām an-Nubalāʾ*. n.p.: Muʾassasat ar-Risālah, 1405/1985.

Fasawī, Yaʿqūb ibn Sufyān. *Al-Maʿrifah wa ʾt-Tārīkh*. Beirut: Muʾassasat ar-Risālāh, 1401/1981.

Gangohī, Rashīd Aḥmad. *Al-Kawkab ad-Durrī ʿalāʾ Jāmiʿ at-Tirmidhī*. Karachi: Idārat al-Qurʾān, 1407/1987.

Ḥākim, Muḥammad ibn ʿAbdillāh Abū ʿAbdillāh. *Al-Mustadrak ʿalā aṣ-Ṣaḥīḥayn*. Beirut: Dār al-Kutub al-ʿIlmiyyah, 1411/1990.

Haythamī, Nūr ad-Dīn. *Majmaʿ az-Zawāʾid*. Cairo: Maktabat al-Qudsī, 1414/1994.

Ḥumaydī, Abū Bakr. *Musnad al-Ḥumaydī*. Damascus: Dār as-Saqā, 1996.

Ibn ʿAbd al-Barr, Abū ʿUmar. *Al-Istidhkār al-Jāmiʿ li-Madhāhib Fuqahāʾ al-Amṣār wa ʿUlamāʾ al-Aqṭār*. Beirut: Dār al-Kutub al-ʿIlmiyyah, 2000 /1421.

Ibn Abī Ḥātim, ʿAbd ar-Raḥmān. *Al-Jarḥ wa't-Taʿdīl*. Hyderabad: Ṭabʿat Majlis Dāʾirat al-Maʿārif al-ʿUthmāniyyah, 1271/1952.

Ibn Abī Ḥātim, ʿAbd ar-Raḥmān. *Tafsīr al-Qurʾān al-ʿAẓīm*. Saudi Arabia: Maktabat Nazzār Muṣṭafā al-Bāz, 1419/1998.

Ibn Abī ad-Dunyā, Abū Bakr. *Muḥāsabat an-Nafs*. Beirut: Dār al-Kutub al-ʿIlmiyyah, 1406/1986.

Ibn ʿAdī, Abū Aḥmad. *Al-Kāmil fī Ḍuʿafāʾ ar-Rijāl*. Beirut: Dār al-Kutub al-ʿIlmiyyah, 1418/1997.

Ibn Baṭṭāl al-Mālikī, Abū 'l-Ḥasan. *Sharḥ Ṣaḥīḥ al-Bukhārī*. Riyad: Maktabat ar-Rushd, 1423/2003.

Ibn Ḥanbal, Aḥmad. *Zuhd*. Beirut: Dār al-Kutub al-ʿIlmiyyah, 1420/1999.

Ibn Ḥanbal, Aḥmad. *Musnad al-Imām Aḥmad ibn Ḥanbal*. Beirut: Mu'assasat ar-Risālāh, 1421/2001.

Ibn Ḥibbān al-Bustī, Muḥammad. *Majrūḥīn*. Aleppo: Dār al-Waʿī, 1396 /1976.

Ibn Ḥibbān al-Bustī, Muḥammad. *Ṣaḥīḥ Ibn Ḥibbān*. Beirut: Mu'assasat ar-Risālah, 1408/1988.

Ibn Hubayrah, Yaḥyā. *Al-Ifṣāḥ ʿan Maʿānī aṣ-Ṣiḥāḥ*. Riyad: Dār al-Waṭan, 1417/1996.

Ibn al-Jawzī, ʿAbd ar-Raḥmān. *Kashf al-Mushkil min Ḥadīth as-Ṣaḥīḥayn*. Riyad: Dār al-Waṭan, n.d.

Ibn al-Jawzī, ʿAbd ar-Raḥmān. *Al-Muntaẓam fī Tārīkh al-Umam wa 'l-Mulūk*. Beirut: Dār al-Kutub al-ʿIlmiyyah, 1412/1992.

Ibn Khuzaymah, Abū Bakr Muḥammad ibn Isḥāq. *Ṣaḥīḥ Ibn Khuzaymah*. Beirut: Al-Maktab al-Islāmī, 1970.

Ibn Mājah, ʿAbdullāh Muḥammad ibn Yazīd al-Qazwīnī. *Sunan Ibn Mājah*. Beirut: Dār al-Fikr, n.d.

Ibn Mufliḥ, Shams ad-Dīn. *Al-Ādāb al-Sharʿiyyah wa 'l-Minaḥ al-Marʿiyyah*. Beirut: Dār ʿĀlam al-Kutub, n.d.

Ibn al-Mundhir, Abū Bakr. *Ijmāʿ*. Saharanpur: Al-Maktabah al-Asʿadiyyah, n.d.

Ibn al-Qayyim, Muḥammad ibn Abī Bakr. *Zād al-Maʿād fī Hady Khayr al-ʿIbād*. Beirut: Mu'assasat ar-Risālah, 1415/1994.

Ibn Qutaybah, Abū Muḥammad. *Ta'wīl Mukhtalif al-Ḥadīth*. Beirut: Al-Maktab al-Islāmī, 1419/1999.

Ibn Rāhūyah, Isḥāq. *Musnad Isḥāq ibn Rāhūyah*. Madīnah: Maktabat al-Īmān, 1412/1991.

Ibn Rajab, Zayn ad-Dīn. *Fatḥ al-Bārī*. Madīnah: Maktabat al-Gurabā' al-Athariyyah, 1417/1996.

Ibn Saʿd, Abū ʿAbdillāh Muḥammad. *Aṭ-Ṭabaqāt al-Kubrā*. Beirut: Dār al-Kutub al-ʿIlmiyyah, 1410/1990.

Ibn Shabbah, ʿUmar. *Tārīkh al-Madīnah*. n.p.: n.p., n.d.

Ibn Taymiyyah, Aḥmad ibn ʿAbd al-Ḥalīm. *Iqtiḍāʾ aṣ-Ṣirāṭ al-Mustaqīm*. Beirut: Dār ʿĀlam al-Kutub, 1419/1999.

Ibn Taymiyyah, Aḥmad ibn ʿAbd al-Ḥalīm. *Majmūʿ al-Fatāwā*. Madīnah: Majmaʿ al-Malik Fahad li-Ṭabāʿat al-Musḥaf ash-Sharīf, 1416/1995.

ʿIyāḍ al-Mālikī, Abu ʾl-Faḍl. *Ikmāl al-Muʿlim bi-Fawāʾid Muslim*. Cairo: Dār al-Wafā li ʾṭ-Ṭabāʿah wa ʾn-Nashr wa ʾt-Tawzīʿ, 1419/1998.

Jazarī, Mubārak ibn Muḥammad. *An-Nihāyah fī Gharīb al-Ḥadīth wa ʾl-Athar*. Beirut: Al-Maktabah al-ʿIlmiyyah, 1399/1979.

Khaṭṭābī, Abū Sulaymān. *Maʿālim as-Sunan Sharḥ Sunan Abī Dāwūd*. Aleppo: Al-Maṭbaʿah al-ʿIlmiyyah, 1351/1932.

Khaṭṭābī, Abū Sulaymān. *Sharḥ Ṣaḥīḥ al-Bukhārī*. Makkah: Umm al-Qura University, 1409/1988.

Khaṭīb al-Baghdādī, Abū Bakr Aḥmad ibn ʿAlī. *Tarīkh Baghdād*. Beirut: Dār al-Kutub al-ʿIlmiyyah, 1417/1996.

Kirmānī, Shams ad-Dīn. *Al-Kawākib ad-Dirārī fī Sharḥ Ṣaḥīḥ al-Bukhārī*. Beirut: Dār Iḥyāʾ at-Turāth al-ʿArabī, 1401/1981.

Mizzī, Jamāl ad-Dīn. *Tahdhīb al-Kamāl fī Asmāʾ ar-Rijāl*. Beirut: Muaʾssasat ar-Risālah, 1400/1980.

Munāwī, ʿAbd ar-Raʾūf. *Fayḍ al-Qadīr Sharḥ al-Jāmiʿ aṣ-Ṣaghīr*. Egypt: Al-Maktabah at-Tijāriyyah al-Kubrā, 1356/1937.

Muslim ibn al-Ḥajjāj. *Ṣaḥīḥ Muslim*. Beirut: Dār Iḥyāʾ at-Turāth al-ʿArabī, n.d.

Nasaʿī, Abū ʿAbd ar-Raḥmān Aḥmad ibn Shuʿayb ibn ʿAlī. *Al-Mujtabā min as-Sunan*. Aleppo: Maktabat al-Maṭbūʿāt al-Islāmiyyah, 1406/1986.

Nasaʾī, Abū ʿAbd al-Raḥmān Aḥmad ibn Shuʿayb ibn ʿAlī. *As-Sunan al-Kubrā*. Beirut: Muaʾssasat ar-Risālah, 1421/2001.

Nawawī, Abū Zakarīyyah Yaḥyā ibn Sharaf. *Al-Minhāj fī Sharḥ Ṣaḥīḥ Muslim ibn al-Ḥajjāj*. Beirut: Dār Iḥyāʾ at-Turāth al-ʿArabī, 1392/1972.

Qārī, ʿAlī ibn Sulṭān Muḥammad. *Mirqāt al-Mafātīḥ Sharḥ Mishkāt al-Maṣābīḥ*. Beirut: Dār al-Fikr, 1422/2002.

Shaybānī, Muḥammad ibn al-Ḥasan. *Muwaṭṭaʾ*, published with Laknawī, Muḥammad ʿAbd al-Ḥayy. *At-Taʿlīq al-Mumajjad ʿalā Muwaṭṭaʾ Muḥammad*. Damascus: Dār al-Qalam, 1426/2005.

Ṭabarānī, Abu 'l-Qāsim Sulaymān ibn Aḥmad. *Al-Mu'jam al-Awsaṭ*. Cairo: Dār al-Ḥaramayn, 1415/1994.

Ṭabarānī, Abu 'l-Qāsim Sulaymān ibn Aḥmad. *Al-Mu'jam al-Kabīr*. Cairo: Maktabat Ibn Taymiyyah, 1415/1994.

Ṭabarānī, Abu 'l-Qāsim Sulaymān ibn Aḥmad. *Musnad ash-Shāmiyyīn*. Beirut: Mu'assasat ar-Risālah, 1405/1984.

Ṭabarī, Muḥammad ibn Jarīr. *Jāmi' al-Bayān*. Cairo: Dār Hijr, 1422/2001.

Ṭaḥāwī, Abū Ja'far Aḥmad ibn Muḥammad. *Sharḥ Mushkil al-Āthār*. Beirut: Mu'assasat ar-Risālah, 1415/1994.

Tirmidhī, Muḥammad ibn 'Īsā. *Al-Jāmi' al-Kabīr*. Beirut: Dār Iḥyā' at-Turāth al-'Arabī, n.d.

Tūribishtī, Faḍlullāh. *Al-Muyassar fī Sharḥ Maṣābīḥ as-Sunnah*. Saudi Arabia: Maktabat Nazzār Muṣṭafā al-Bāz, 1429/2008.

'Uthmānī, Shabīr Aḥmad. *Fatḥ al-Mulhim*. Damascus: Dār al-Qalam, 1427/2006.

Wakī' ibn al-Jarrāḥ. *Zuhd*. Madīnah: Maktabat ad-Dār, 1404/1984.